Life and Traditions
of the Ribble Valley

THE RIBCHESTER
PARADE HELMET.

**Ribblesdale and Bowland
books by W R Mitchell**

BOWLAND AND PENDLE HILL
LANCASHIRE WITCH COUNTRY
THE LOST VILLAGE OF STOCKS-IN-BOWLAND
STOCKS RE-VISITED
PENDLE AND THE TROUGH
HELLIFIELD AND THE RAILWAY
EXPLORING THE RIBBLE VALLEY

Life and Traditions of the Ribble Valley

by W R Mitchell

Bolton-by-Bowland

CASTLEBERG
1994

For
SHIRLEY BROADHURST
of Kaydee Books,
Clitheroe.

A **Castleberg** Book.

First published in the United Kingdom in 1994.

Copyright © W R Mitchell 1994.

The moral right of the author has been asserted.

ISBN 1 871064 98 8

Typeset in Palacio, printed and bound in the
United Kingdom by Lamberts Printers,
Station Road, Settle, North Yorkshire, BD24 9AA.

Published by Castleberg, 18 Yealand Avenue, Giggleswick,
Settle, North Yorkshire, BD24 0AY.

Contents

Illustrations

Photography by the Author
    Front cover: Downham. Back cover: Stonyhurst College.
Drawings:
    Richard Bancroft, 6, 11, 15, 19, 29, 31, 54, 55, 63, 65, 70, 78, 95, 105, 113, 117
    Peter Fox, 22, 45, 61, 92.
Map by David Leather.

Clitheroe.

Foreword

by Tony Jackson, Mayor of Ribble Valley (1993-4)

RIBBLESDALE stretches from Ribblehead to the coastal marshes near St Annes-on-Sea. The area covered by Bill Mitchell's book is confined, however, to the Borough of Ribble Valley, extending from Gisburn to Ribchester and bounded on either side by Pendle Hill and the Bowland Fells.

The largest borough in Lancashire, Ribble Valley is twenty years young, having been founded with the amalgamation of a number of Rural and Urban District Councils in 1974. There came into being a local government area of 230 square miles, of which 70 per cent consists of an Area of Outstanding Natural Beauty. Within those square miles there are more sheep than people!

Bill Mitchell, a much respected naturalist and author, edited *The Dalesman* for many years until his retirement in 1988. We first met many years ago as members of an organisation committed to the well-being of Bowland's largest mammal, the sika deer.

Journey with Bill as he takes us to meet the people of Ribble Valley, their history and traditions. As you read this book, I hope you will realise why I love this Valley of ours and why I was so delighted to have been asked to write a foreword. I am sure the reader who follows this literary excursion will realise what a special place it is—and why so many people hold it dear.

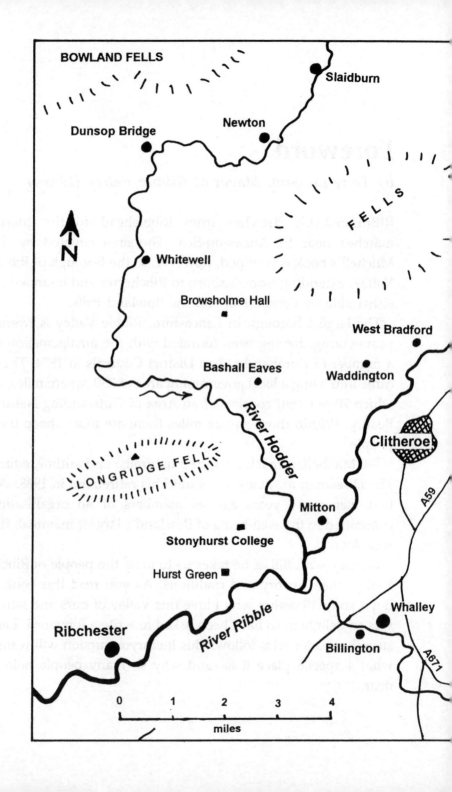

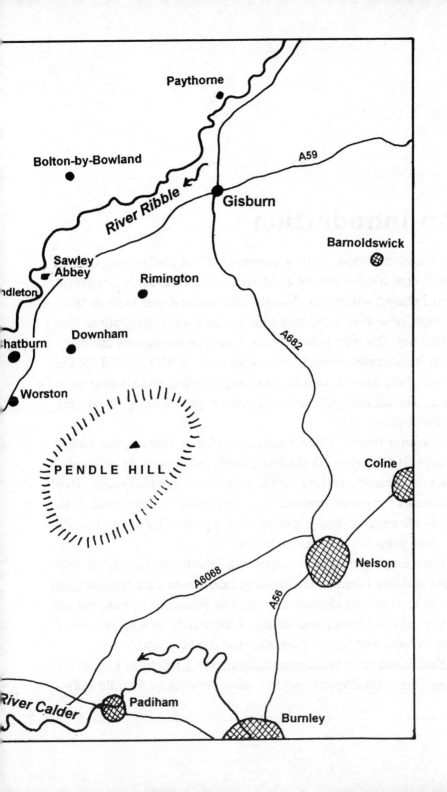

An Introduction

LIFE and tradition. Both were evident last December, when I conducted a carol service at Mount Sion, Tosside, a Congregational chapel which has changed little since it was built in 1812, though now it is used but four times a year. The stove was white-hot; the woodwork creaked and the big square building, with its stepped gallery, was dimly lit, which added to the sense of mystery. When the reading, praying and singing were over, we all enjoyed tea and mince pies before dispersing under a starry sky.

Not long before, I had taken a service at Harrop, the oldest chapel in Clitheroe Methodist circuit, where—as at Tosside— the present and a feeling for the past blend harmoniously. This diminutive place of worship, situated beside a farm road, with fields all around, has a gallery and a pulpit big enough for a restless preacher to pace about in.

The congregation of a dozen was made up largely of folk from scattered farms. The heating came from a cherry-red coal fire in an ordinary domestic grate. The music for hymn-singing was produced by a harmonium. Afterwards, at a local farm, I was entertained to an old-fashioned country tea.

New ideas soon become traditional. On Christmas Eve, at Fir Tree Farm, Rimington—within easy viewing of Pendle Hill—

West Bradford.

the Nativity was re-enacted in a barn by the light of paraffin lamps. The parts of Mary, Joseph and the Christ Child, were played by a young couple and their baby. Young people provided musical accompaniment for the carol singing. Donkey, sheep and lambs had been mustered. The congregation sat on bales of hay.

The churchfolk at Gisburn, inspired by their vicar (the Rev Jonathan Lumby) indulged in "hugging" on Mothering Sunday. They were "giving t'owd church a hug, not ourselves." Joining hands, they formed a human chain around the building. "The first time we did it, a man from the Kennels stood on the tower and when t'last hands were clasped, he blew on his hunting horn.''

Elsewhere, at an animal service, the congregation was accompanied by goats, a budgie, dogs and cats. ''Outside the church was a pen holding a calf. A little girl brought a piglet. The marvellous thing was how quiet it was. Not a yap or a squeal was heard.''

Life in the Ribble Valley and Bowland has a homeliness which springs from an awareness of the past, as was evident when former Daleheaders thronged the Institute at Tosside for a slide show I gave for the funds of Dalehead Church. I talked my way back down the years. When there was some doubt about the age of a photograph of a group of women, one of whom was holding a baby, a man rose stiffly to his feet and said: ''It was nineteen fourteen—I'se t'babby!''

An example of what I call ''living history'' concerns a Chatburn man who told me about the former mill (recently demolished). A textile mill gives the impression of being truly old, yet when the big chimney had been built as part of an extension, over seventy years before, he and his mother were among those who had the rare privilege of being raised to the chimney top in the wooden tub which was hitherto used for taking up men and materials.

Standing at the rim of the chimney, mother and son enjoyed a novel view of the park-like valley, flanked by the Bowland Fells and Pendle Hill.

When I stood with a party of visitors in the great library at Stonyhurst College, a Jesuit priest reviewed the history of the collection. He updated the story by recalling that the count took place here for an important by-election. Holding up his right hand, this unpretentious, scholarly man remarked, with a mischievous smile, that it had shaken the hand of Screaming

Lord Such.

A Ribble Valley landowner, questioned about Lord Ribblesdale, of Gisburne Park, who died in 1925, not only remembered this celebrity—he had occasionally gone riding with him. And he also remembered the Ormerod brothers who, with Ribblesdale, had introduced sika deer to the district as a quarry for the Buckhounds. The hounds died out many years ago; the deer remain and have been joined by roe deer spreading here via the Lune and Wenning valleys.

It amuses me that the Ribble Valley, so often thought of as being "a bit of old England" should have in its fauna sika deer (of a species which evolved in the Japanese archipelago) and pheasant (bred from Asian jungle fowl). The rhododendrons which were planted round so many fine halls in the Valley were also introduced from Asia.

Pillars from the Roman fort at Ribchester prop up the stone porch of a local inn. At Whalley, cars on a byroad are driven through the arch of a monastic gatehouse. An arch from old Sawley Abbey once obtruded on to the highway but now provides a venerable gateway for—a local field. The Ribble flows clear and cool between banks which, by and large, remain unspoilt by unsightly development.

A church on a limestone ridge peeps across river, field and copse to mighty Pendle. A Georgian hall presides over an unbesmirched landscape of green hillocks. A seventeenth century hall, with rows of mullion windows and a roof of local slate, is now a farmhouse, with a collie dog kennelled near the back door.

The Ribble Valley has its legends, none of which stand up to serious study. Even dear old Wada, who is supposed to have given his name to Waddington, may not have existed in the heroic form mentioned today.

A wily squire, William Pudsay of Bolton, was a coiner, using silver from his mine near Rimington to make shillings. The law caught up with him but he appears to have been pardoned. What remains is pure romance—that William, short of money, met some fairies who gave him a magic bit for his horse.

The fairies also told Pudsay that if he dug at a certain spot near Rimington, he would discover silver. When he became a coiner, to make a quick fortune, and he was about to be arrested at Bolton Hall, he mounted his horse and (presumably making full use of the magic bit) they leapt off Rainsber Scar (the old name for what is now called Pudsay's Leap) and survived.

Life and tradition were well-illustrated at Browsholme Hall in July, 1993, when Eleanor Constance Parker was born, daughter of Robert and Amanda Parker, a family associated with the locality for many centuries and with Browsholme Hall (pronounce it Broos'm) since this gentleman's residence was built in 1507.

The proud father was reported in the *Clitheroe Advertiser* as saying: "In the historical context, it's exciting to have a baby here for the first time since 1857. It's a very friendly house. There are no ghosts, no secret passages. But the family and Eleanor will need a lot of energy on a day-to-day basis to keep Browsholme going. She'll be a busy girl."

Life and Traditions in the Ribble Valley is neither a guide book or a reference work for walkers. It simply describes a magnificent tract of landscape and relates a variety of folk tales, some old and some not so old.

When I first began to record them, Yorkshire claimed the major part of Bowland and had a common boundary with Lancashire on stretches of the river Ribble. Since 1974, virtually all the area reviewed has been under the emblem of the Red Rose.

The best way to get to know a parish is to "beat the bounds", as was the case before accurate maps were printed. Every ten years or so, the young people were made familiar with features of the boundary by being walked around the parish and being beaten at certain points so they were "bound" to remember it.

It was supposed to be done in a day, but at Gisburn: "Our parish boundary is thirty-six miles long. We beat the bounds in three sessions—twelve miles a time." Tradition or no tradition, modern youngsters would not take kindly to being thrashed.

Trinity Youth and Community Centre

Down The Ribble

THE RIBBLE, some sixty-five miles long, rises on the Yorkshire Pennines, flows southwards and then turns west to join the Irish Sea at Preston.

I'm fascinated by the Ribble. On my early morning walk, I cross it twice—on a footbridge at the Locks, Langcliffe, where I am in the company of dipper and kingfisher, then at Settle Bridge, where a grey heron awaits its fish breakfast.

At each place, the river pours over a weir which used to inhibit the movement of salmonid (salmon and sea trout) on their spawning runs. They needed a pool from which to spring. The answer was to instal a "ladder", a series of pools, at each weir. The fish now have the whole Ribble system available to them. When, in late summer, my eye catches a flash of silver as a salmon leaps on to the lower rung of this curious ladder, I marvel that any have survived the centuries of predation by man, who netted them by the hundred.

The name Ribble is said to be derived from a word meaning "boundary". Could this long watercourse have been called because it was the division between two Anglian kingdoms? Students of dialect are aware of the Ribble as a division between old forms of speech. South of the river, a hill is an "edge" and to the north the old Norse word "fell" applies.

When the Normans were consolidating their hold on England, what is now Cumbria was held by David, the Scottish King. The Scots were soon pushed back. In Domesday Book, land between the Ribble and Mersey, which was to become part of Lancashire, was included in a section headed *Terra inter Ripam et Mersham*, while to the north of the Ribble lay the diocese of York, extending from sea to sea.

In early wireless days, weather forecasters speaking from Manchester were fond of referring to conditions north or south of the Ribble. People living south of the river were once known as O'er Ribblers. An osprey, seen flying over the Ribble near Great Mitton was claimed for both Yorkshire and Lancashire and was duly mentioned in the ornithological records of each county.

This great river is relatively clean and, coming off the limestone, very productive, though a landowner mentioned such general pollutants as acid rain and, in a farming valley, "all this bagged fertiliser and slurry they pour on to the fields, some of which is washed into the streams and the river."

I have listened to dozens of arguments about where the source of the Ribble lies. The Ribble Way opts for the source of the highest of the feeder becks, at about 1,850 ft. Walkers are enticed by dotted lines on a map, filling their feet with bog water on their way to Jam Sike and Gavel Gap.

I favour, as the source of the Ribble, that of the longest tributary, which is Gayle Beck, emanating from the southern slope of Wold Fell (more precisely, Newby Head Moss) where (I hasten to add) there is no public right of way.

Wold Fell was acknowledged as the source by A T R Houghton, "late Clerk to the Ribble Board of Conservators", who in 1952 had a much-respected history of the Ribble Salmon Fisheries published. He wrote, with quiet authority: "There is a small beck crossing the road through a culvert, having its source in a spring a short distance up Wold Fell. That spring is the source of the Ribble.''

Houghton mentions that the beck is joined by other becks or gills "and presently becomes Gayle Beck, in which there are beds of gravel suitable for spawning fish as high up as its junction with Long Gill on Gayle Moor.'' Gayle Beck, so often dry during spring droughts, flows near a shooting box. The oyster-catcher, a pied bird with a bill like a stick of red sealing wax, nests on the shingle.

In Thorn's Gill, the cold fell water has cut deeply into limestone, creating a mini-ravine. The abrasive action of small stones has eroded "potholes" which, though small, are deep and round. The beck flows under a single-span packhorse bridge which has metal splints to preserve it until remedial work can be done. Gayle Beck now assumes the name of Ribble, being joined by a beck from Ribblehead, which is dominated by a 24-arch viaduct of the Settle-Carlisle Railway.

North Ribblesdale was deepened and smoothed in glacial times. Fingers of ice, emanating from Lakeland, scoured the area. When the ice melted, drumlin fields (composed of many smooth heaps of glacial debris which on the map resemble basketfuls of eggs were created). The lowest part of the valley near Selside is still quite marshy. Hereabouts, the Ribble is joined by Cam Beck, which flows from limestone country and has abundant food for the native trout.

At Stainforth Foss, just below a famous packhorse bridge, the water tumbles over a cill of gritstone. The hand of man has subtly re-shaped the natural rock. The River Authority, after much wrangling with the Dales Park planning authority, and the expenditure of a few thousand pounds, sculpted the rock, improving the salmon's changes of negotiating the fall.

West Bradford.

At Settle, a brawling river pours over a weir and dashes itself against Queen's Rock, a feature on a major geological fault. Now it enters the Ribble Valley—a wide, shallow valley, once the bed of a glacial lake and now consisting of peaty ground over gravel.

Here are the Long Preston Deeps, where the Ribble swirls and bubbles between soundproofed banks which are over-run after periods of heavy rain, restoring to the Ribble its lake appearance. The Deeps are more typical of a river near its estuary than one in the upper reaches. The old Fylde Water Board had hoped to convert the valley into a river-regulating reservoir. A dam would have been built where the water uses a gap between glacial moraines—a gap which is so narrow it is like the neck of a bottle. Comparatively little concrete would have been needed to "cork" the bottle.

More of the egg-shaped drumlins are common between Hellfield and Gisburn. By its shape, a drumlin indicates the direction in which the ice flowed. At Nappa, stepping stones enable the walker to cross dry-shod, except when the river is in spate. A pre-bridge causeway of dressed stone is still to be seen on the bed of the river at Paythorne.

Then the dale opens out. The Ribble passes Clitheroe and receives an infusion of fresh water from the Hodder, the main watercourse of Bowland. Preston "milked" the Hodder of over one-fifth of its waters; the less water there is to clean up any pollution, the worse that pollution becomes, though the Hodder remains a good river for brown trout, sea trout and salmon.

Between Hodder Foot and Calder Foot, anglers are more common than farmers. Riverside platforms are evident. Neat wooden shelters with seats are seen at regular intervals on the river bank. A landowner lamented that the Ribble, once one of the best trout and grayling rivers in the North, now has comparatively few "wild" trout and few riparian owners who themselves fish the water. "Instead they let it to angling associations, who stock it with hatchery trout."

A ripple of excitement passes along both sides of the river when the salmon are running. Fish which hatched out in the Ribble, and migrated to deep waters off Greenland and the Faroes to feed up, return to their natal river, driven by the urge to propagate their kind.

Spawning in the Ribble occurs in late November and December, and on the Hodder the season is from the middle of December through to early January. Sea trout penetrate further into the river system than salmon, reaching small becks at the head of the Hodder catchment.

The female salmon makes a depression in the gravel and here lays her eggs, some nine hundred eggs for every pound of her weight, the eggs being fertilised by an attendant male salmon, which looks fearsome with a bony hook on the lower law. Modern research indicates that some hen fish lay eggs in more than one redd, with—in some cases—another cock fish in attendance.

Maybe no more than four or five per cent of eggs hatch out and few fish reach maturity. Redds may be washed out by severe floods or destroyed by "overcutting", when the spot is chosen by another salmon and the first eggs are disturbed. In dry weather, redds dry out. Salmon eggs are tasty morsels for birds like goosander, heron, gull and cormorant. To a resident brown trout, salmon eggs are a delectable meal.

The River Authority's hatchery near Dunsop Bridge produces salmon and sea trout for re-stocking. At Waddow Weir is a fish trap, used for collecting brood stock at the end of the season. The latest type of fish counter has been installed at Waddow and Winkley (on the Hodder) and at Locks (near Langcliffe, on the Ribble).

The Ribble and Hodder are "late" rivers judging by the numbers of fish caught by anglers. The spring (February to April) run of fish is not large. Relatively few salmon are hooked between May and July. The main season for angling is from August to October, given a good flow of water in the river.

Mr Houghton, already quoted, mentioned Hodder Foot as a feature to be treated with respect. "Here there is a deep hole with rocky ledges ending in sheer drops into the depths below, and more than one keen angler, striving to covert the pool, has stepped forward on to nothing but water and found himself swimming for his life!"

The "Mid Ribble", as it has now become, some forty-five miles from its source, accepts the Calder, which has become sweeter in recent years. Forty years ago, Mr Houghton and his friends were conscious of "a kind of antiseptic smell; now we notice a visible line where the two streams join; the Ribble clean and bright and full of larvae and other fish food, the

Calder dark and almost barren...A sudden thunderstorm in East Lancashire in early summer can bring Calder down in a black flood, choking all fish for many miles below."

Major Yorke, who presided over the Ribble Fisheries Association in the 1920s, confirms this. "When the Calder came down in flood, there was a filthy wave of pollution from all the factories. It choked every fish from there to Bamber Bridge. When the Ribble and Hodder were full, they swept away the mess the Calder was bringing down."

He acknowledges that the National River Authority have cleaned up the river and is delighted to hear of fish being caught at Calder Foot. The augmented Ribble flows under Ribchester Bridge, which is a mile above the village of that name. Near Preston, the Ribble blends its water with the sea.

Dunsop Bridge, on the Hodder.

Halton West and Nappa

> ...the four little Yorkes ran in and out, into the
> garden, out to their ponies in the stables, down
> to the river to play or paddle or fish.
>
> *Anne Ashley Cooper in "Yorke
> Country" (1988).*

IN THE Domesday Book of 1086 AD, it is noted that Roger de
Poitou owned 180 taxable cultivated acres at Halton, an attractive part of the Ribble Valley which was given to the Church—
in this case, to Bolton Priory—by a Norman lord who had fared
well in this world and wanted to take out some form of
insurance against calamity in the next.

Halton West, which remains a small community, stands on
high ground above the Ribble, which is spanned by a substantial stone bridge. Bolton Priory—it was never an Abbey—
established a grange at Halton and augmented the local labour
force when the corn was due to be harvested.

Early in the fourteenth century, a time of persistent Scottish
raids, the farm routine was fitful. In 1318, the Halton grange
was destroyed. The de Halton family were tenants of Bolton
until 1485, when a heiress married into the Talbot family. In
due course, and after several changes of ownership, Thomas

Yorke, a bachelor lawyer, bought Halton from Edmund Munday in 1737.

Thomas built Halton Place, a splendid Georgian house on a ridge overlooking the Ribble, in 1770. John Crunden, the architect, designed a brick structure, faced with stone, contriving that the view from the large windows took the eye up the Ribble Valley to Ingleborough and Penyghent. Southwards, the sparkling Ribble is seen flowing between the soft green forms of the drumlins.

When Thomas married Jane, the daughter of Joseph Reay, of Killingworth, Northumberland, Halton Place became the elder son's dower-house, associated with the Yorke family's major estate, at Bewerley, near Pateley Bridge. Anne Ashley-Cooper, daughter of Major and Mrs Yorke, in her book entitled *Yorke Country* (1988) gives the flavour of the times when Thomas and Jane presided over Halton Place. She mentions the farm work, the droves of Scotch cattle—black Galloways and Highland kyloes—passing down Ribblesdale on their way to Lancashire.

The young couple were driven to Long Preston church and allocated some time to visiting the neighbours. The packman brought more than just muslins, holland, laces and ribbons—''he brought excitement for he carried news from the outside world, patent medicines for ague or rheumatism, political comment, the latest fashion tips and the newest song.''

The Yorkes maintain Halton Place's status as a private home in an age when many such country houses have been converted to other uses or, indeed, have become derelict. Major Yorke, despite blindness, contrives to fish in the Ribble. A friend puts out the line and Major Yorke continues the angling process ''through force of habit''.

His daughter, Anne, recalling her young days at Halton, notes that at every season of the year, the height and condition of the water was a daily topic. "My father, with a fisherman's eye, would say happily, 'Good water today', or less cheerfully, 'Far too big', 'Too brown' or 'Too low'. My mother was also a keen fisherman, but her special joy was to watch the dippers, kingfishers, oyster catchers, mallard, curlews and the occasional sandpiper. For us children, the river was a living, always changing friend."

Major Yorke's sharp memory retains details of every variation in the bed of the Ribble—the stretches of shallow water, with wadeable pools, and the deep pools, one of which, under Halton Bridge, has a depth of seventeen feet.

A modern feature of the river is the rapid alternation of low and high water. "In the old days, a good water lasted five days...Now it goes down, or comes up, four feet in a night. The fish don't like that."

Ribble was full of beautiful brown trout, each of about three-quarters of a pound in weight. "If you looked under a wood on a really hot summer's day, you would see ten or twelve fish swim out from the shade of the trees. You don't now." The grayling come and go. They went off some years ago and now they are coming back and the river holds a nice stock of fish.

In the 1930s, there was a run of long, thin salmon; good fish nonetheless, with a weight of around 15 lb to 16 lb. "They were always late coming, so the fisheries board introduced some fish with a larger girth from northern Scotland. The best season for catching these fish was (and still is) July, August and into September. The sport was very much improved."

In the 1960s, disease wiped out the stock and it took three or four years to get it back again. Now, with field pollution and the rapid rise and fall of the water, the salmon run through to Stainforth and Horton-in-Ribblesdale, where the land has beef cattle and sheep. There is no slurry to seep into the river.

"Down here, we did not have a single pull on the line in the 1993 season."

When in his early teens, Major Yorke used to ride his pony over to Gisburne Park, he joined Lord Ribblesdale, who was mounted on a fine horse. As they rode, the bailiff went in front to open the gates and his groom rode behind, to shut them. "Lord Ribblesdale was rather silent in the mornings. Then he'd suddenly say: 'That is my idea of a good Shorthorn'. We would look at the cow and then at his woods. He was very kind to me though in general he was a sad, morose man, having lost both his sons. His beloved wife had died of TB. "When you got him going, he always had something worth while to say."

Having lived through the technological revolution on the land, Major Yorke can look back on more laborious ways of farming—on "old pastures, limed and slagged; meadows well-mucked: little round hummocks of muck dragged from the old red cart, then scaled with a flick of the fork."

Nappa—mentioned in the Domesday Book as Nappay—was then the home of 26 people, compared with 11 today. Nine-tenths of its history concerns a quiet pastoral way of life. The old farms had their water-meadows, from which the land rose to encompass drumlins. From the highest ground at Nappa is a grand view through 360 degrees.

Nappa was important as a crossing point of the river. It is said to have been used by the Romans. Mary Stewart, the best-selling novelist, in a trilogy of books about King Arthur, used Nappa as the site of one of the twelve battles he is said to have fought when journeying northwards. She re-named the river Ribble, calling it "Tribuit". Nappa is mentioned in an appendix to her book. The present road spends much of its time out of sight of the Ribble and, its line determined in the turnpike days of the 18th century, it is still referred to as the "new" road.

At Nappa, in recent times, three historic islands were bulldozed and obliterated. An old man told me that one island was "like a gurt field". George Bargh, the third generation of his family to farm at Nappa, recalls that the largest of the three lost islands lay near the Halton West bank; the others were claimed by the parish of Nappa.

Thus the river was split into three channels, with stepping stones extending to the largest island, which was crossed by a path, the stones continuing on the other side. These islands are clearly shown on a map of the parish of Gisburn drawn "for the commutation of tithes". The details were taken in 1844 from the Ordnance Survey and the map signed by Captain E W Dunford, of the Royal Engineers.

George took me down to the river, where some of the stepping stones are now in need of attention. We walked through scrubland on the Nappa bank which resembles the type of vegetation found on the islands. In the 1940s, a cold snap froze the water to a depth of ten inches and the thaw was dramatic. Hearing a tremendous crash, George's mother looked from the kitchen window at seventeenth century Nappa Manor Farm and saw that the ice had begun to move. When it hit the stepping stones and the islands, it piled up.

Huge icefloes were swept on to the banking. Some of the stepping stones, each about a cubic yard, had been pushed to the bottom end of the islands over a hundred yards downriver. "Great lumps of ice littered the banking for weeks."

Among the diverse range of plants which grew on the islands were primroses, wood anemones, spring onions, red currants and gooseberries. George said: "The grass was so high we called it 'elephant grass'. You could get lost in it. The islands had trees big enough for us to climb them." Thrifty farmers mowed the islands by scythe and made hay. The big island was the prerogative of Joss Moorhouse, who farmed Nappa Flatts.

The Barghs took hay from the two islands to the east. "We never considered we had finished haymaking until these islands, the roadsides, the railway bankings and some old limestone quarries had been mown with a scythe and made into hay. When it came to the islands, somehow we managed to get the horse-drawn lorry down the side of the banking below the stepping stones so that we could get across and recover the hay. The grass was strong stuff. The hay scratched your arms as you were loading it."

George recalled that "at the time the islands were moved, the children across the river found a kingfisher's nest and showed it to us. It was partly because of that nest we were so angry when this huge excavator came one day and a man told us that 'we've come to move the islands'." The Bargh family remonstrated with the excavator driver, telling him they were going on holiday and mentioning the location of the kingfisher nest. He agreed to leave that piece of bank, giving the young birds a chance to fledge.

"We duly went on our holidays and when we came back, of course, they had put a different man on the excavator and the whole lot had gone...When they'd finished, the Ribble looked like the Suez Canal." The only good thing was that two expanses of gravel appeared at the river sides. The kingfisher did not stand a chance, but a year or two later a pair of oystercatchers nested.

The Sunday nearest to November 20 was designated at Paythorne as "Salmon Sunday", the day on which crowds of people gathered in the hope of seeing the lordly fish passing on their way to spawn.

"If you were lucky, and the water was right, you'd see salmon splashing up the shallows under the bridge. I once watched them at Nappa. It was fascinating to see lots of fins sticking out of the water. A salmon has tremendous power, clattering over the gravel.''

A farmer who had poached a three foot long fish tried to conceal it by putting it under an old Army greatcoat. The kelt [spawned] fish, which sometimes littered the banks, were ''not fit to eat...They had a fungus over them.''

Gisburn and the Park

Gisburn sits astride the busy A.59 road. Cattle dealers throng its weekly auction and make up the crowds at the annual steeplechase.

The Ribble Way, local authority guide (1988).

AT GISBURN, the Ribble begins its white-water dash through a spectacular gorge. It was once was a secret place but it now a well-known stretch of the Ribble Way which, opened on June 1, 1985, is now one of the many "middle-distance" footpaths, though some walkers—noting its seventy-mile length—may reclassify it as "long distance".

Until the early 1940s, Gisburn had a riverside mill, complete with dam, goit and waterwheel. Originally a corn mill, it was adapted as a sawmill in 1911. The Ribble gorge is referred to in the Ribble Way guide as "the peaceful gorge of Chatburn limestone beyond Sawley".

I did much of my deer-watching in this area. At dusk, in October, my spine tingled as a randy stag, having lain up among the rhododendrons, announced its presence to the hinds with three high-pitched squeals, each long and languid, forming a crescent of sound and resembling a whistle when heard from a distance.

Gisburn.

Once, when the low ground lay under mist which looked almost as substantial as cotton wool, a friend who specialises in recording animal noises made it possible for me to follow the sikine activity through headphones.

In calm weather, a sensitive nose detects the "rotten egg" smell from a sulphur well. Another such well is to be found at Fooden. "It comes out of the rock and is icy cold," says a Gisburn man who has family links with Fooden. "I liked the taste. If you bottled it, the taste was lost. At Fooden, cows used to drink it. And a woman out of the town came every year and washed her feet in it. She said it did her good."

31

Mink are the "newest hazard" on the Ribble. "They are devils on fish as well as on all the little birds." Enticing mink to food in wire traps is an effective way to catch them. When minkhounds arrive beside the Ribble, they soon get on the track of a mink but, when hunted, it is always going to ground. A hunt follower says: "You spend a lot of time digging away in roots and holes. You have about ten men with terriers; another with a spade and another with an axe. It's a splendid day out."

Gisburn, which stands well back from the river, is adorned by a Church which has traces of Norman work and some six-hundred-year old figures in stained glass. Catering establishments, including the seventeenth century *Ribblesdale Arms,* began to prosper, early this century, with the coming of the motor charabancs. Gisburn was reckoned to be the half-way point between Leeds and Blackpool.

"Straight after the war, hundreds of motor coaches came through at the week-end. I've seen that big car park at the *Commercial Hotel* (now closed) so full of coaches you couldn't get another on." The A.59 road has been considerably upgraded and at times is like a speedway.

Some of Gisburn's old cottages have cobblestones to set them off. At one of them lives William Saunders, who recalled for me the 1920s, when Gisburn sustained a summer festival, known to local people as the Field Day. The field in question lay near the auction mart. He was one of a large company of Morris Dancers who, under the control of Billy Roberts, evoked the spirit of Old England. The Morris Men (and women) took the dancing very seriously, to judge by old photographs showing over a score of dancers, as smart as soldiers on parade and looking as though they were concentrating hard.

Gisburn had a blacksmith, a cobbler (who travelled in from

Hellifield) and a coal merchant. Also in the village were the offices of the Holden, Slaidburn and District Co-operative Society (the Holden branch was subsequently moved to Bolton-by-Bowland).

Thursday is auction mart day at Gisburn. In the sale ring, one of Richard Turner's men occupies the rostrum, selling stock with a positive spate of words. Undercover pens are thronged with stock. A farmer arrives with Land Rover and high-sided trailer containing his surplus stock. Clutching his cheque book, a dealer scurries to the office to pay for a purchase, for "time's brass, lad."

In the crowd are "calf men" from the East Riding and "dairy men" from Cheshire, Wales and points south. Drovers and some helpers coax newly-bought stock up a ramp into a multi-storey wagon. It's best not to get in the way at Gisburn on market day.

Old-timers relate that cattle were paraded in the main street. The mart, established in 1911, was at first not as popular as that at Hellifield, which was a rail junction. At Gisburn (as at Hellifield) a Temperance Hotel was opened. The hotel-keeper at Gisburn was a Parker. Rose, one of the girls to be employed, married Henry Slater, whose family had long been in service at Gisburne Park. She in her turn found employment there.

In the not-so-old days, beef breeds which passed through the Gisburn sale ring were Hereford and Angus. The dairy cattle which had been of the Shorthorn breed were succeeded by Friesians. The sheep on offer were Swardles [Swaledales] and "hawf bred 'uns".

Today, there's a strong Continential influence, the beef breeds including the Friesian (originally from the Low Countries) and also Charolais, Simmental and Belgian Blue. Old and trusty beasts like the Herefords and "black pollies" [Aberdeen

Angus) have kept their popularity. They sell a beef animal every half minute—six hundred beasts in a day. "I wouldn't like to guess how many sheep go through the ring." The breeds are not as well defined as they were. Mule and Swaledale, crossed with the Suffolk, yield a good commercial strain of sheep. "Texel sheep are coming in now..."

Gisburn does have a peaceful aspect. The riverside is bedecked with splendid trees and the rolling countryside, with its big fields and woods, is far removed in spirit from the modern world. The land is somewhat claggy, being of medium clay, with some huge sunken boulders, a legacy of the Ice Age. When I was deer-watching regularly, I used to adapt the old Cleveland couplet and say: "Ribblesdale in the clay; take two boots, bring one away."

Older farmers recall the war years (1939-45) when some of the land was ploughed to grow oats, the crop being cut, bound into sheaves, stooked in fields for two or three weeks to dry and then put in a rick to await the visit of the threshing machine. "The thresher travelled the district. Farmers helped each other. We bagged our oats and kept the stuff in the big cellar at the farm. It was an arched cellar with benks [stone shelves) dating from the time it was used as a dairy."

A farmer in the Gisburn area recalled, with a laugh, that oats were rolled and used as a cattle feed. His merriment came from recalling the machinery used. "Our roller was driven by a belt connected to an old car. We jacked up the car so we could take one tyre off; we lapped the belt round the rim of the wheel.

Ploughing and re-seeding with grass-strains suited to silage-making has eradicated from this part of the Ribble Valley the rough fields where the sieves rushes were in dense beds. A farmer recalls when a small girl, out riding a pony, had the bonnet blown from her head. She never found it again because of the rank vegetation.

The process of ensiling grass has been speeded up. "These last few years, we finished the first cut before the end of May." The fields have rallied enough for a second cut to be taken in the middle of July, with (sometimes) a third at the end of August or into September. Now a number of farmers are growing barley to be made into silage—the so-called "whole crop silage"—using a technique that makes it ferment and stops it going mouldy. "It has very high dry matter compared with grass."

Much of the credit for the well-manicured state of the Ribble Valley near Gisburn goes to the Lister family (and their successors, the Lords Ribblesdale). Visitors to Gisburne Park, once the mansion home of the family and now a private hospital, pass between two Gothic entrance lodges and follow a road across a tract of undulating parkland. Here (until 1859) lived a herd of white cattle which had black tips to their noses.

The 3rd Lord Ribblesdale's aversion to having his horses frightened by the new-fangled railway led to the local stretch being set in a tunnel. His Lordship insisted that the portals should be of dressed stone and with castellated turrets. As a native of Gisburn put it: "Lord Ribblesdale forced 'em to make a tunnel." Yet he was the man who cut the first sod of the railway. (The silver spade he used is now to be seen in the museum at Clitheroe Castle). Dashing through the tunnel was a sport young people soon tired of, though courting couples were known to linger there.

The aforementioned Gisburn herd of white cattle, which belonged to the park many years before the toot of the steam locomotive was heard in Ribblesdale, was once as famous as those at Chillingham, in Northumberland. The Gisburn beasts were said to have descended from those kept in the park at Whalley Abbey until the Dissolution, when they were walked to Gisburn, lured (it is said) by music.

The Gisburn stock, weakened by inbreeding, might have been rejuvenated by the blood of the Chillingham stock, but Lord Ribblesdale wanted to keep them pure, with black noses rather than those of reddish colour. The cattle are commemorated by the name of a local inn, the *White Bull*.

Gisburne Park, now a comfortable and well-equipped private hospital, was built by the Listers in 1724 (replacing Low Hall) and it has an original iron fireplace with Italian marble surrounds.

The Lister family settled in the district in 1312 when John married Isabel, daughter and heir of John de Bolton, who was bow-bearer of Bowland. Twenty generations of Listers made their mark on English life. Sir Matthew Lister became President of the Royal College of Physicians. Sir Martin Lister was physician to Queen Anne.

Thomas Lister, elevated to the Peerage in 1797, was the third generation of his family to have represented Clitheroe in Parliament. This intensely patriotic man raised a regiment of Light Dragoons in 1979 and, in 1794, brought into being three troops of Yeomanry. In the American War of Independence, he fitted out (at his own expense) the frigate *Enchantress,* presenting the vessel to the Government.

In days when naval ships had "hearts of oak", the country was ransacked for prime oak with which to build the vessels. It was vital to ensure future supplies. Lord Ribblesdale is said (by Dr Whitaker) to have planted over a million oak trees along the banks of the Ribble, above and below Gisburne Park, "besides an uncounted number of other trees." In 1804, when there was a threat of Napoleonic invasion, this proud man raised the Craven Legion.

From the time he succeeded to his patrimony when he came of age in 1773, he was obsessed with the idea of building a great estate, an early ambition being to ride from Pendle Hill to Malham Tarn on his own property. He beggared himself throughout the whole of his life by attempting something of the kind, despite the fact that he occupied a small property near Dartmouth or elsewhere in Devonshire and resided at Gisburne Park only towards the end of his life. Those who lived at Gisburne Park tasted Ribble salmon in season. In July, 1810, the Hon M Lister killed three "large and most excellent" salmon. It was a good day's work—hardly sport, for he was using a "litster" or leister—a trident with extremely sharp barbs which was plunged into the side of a luckless fish.

His success was accounted for by the fact that Brocka Call or Weir, which spanned the river near Preston, had been accidentally left open. Normally, a vast number of salmon were intercepted there. Young Lister's moment of triumph as a fisherman may have prompted the reigning Lord Ribblesdale to advance the £100, then a further subscription of £50, towards buying Brocka Mill and Weir to "open a free and uninterrupted passage for the salmon and other fish up the river north east of this intolerable nuisance."

When the 4th and last Lord Ribblesdale died in 1925, the folk of Gisburn found themselves without a reigning Lister for the first time in twenty generations. With no living male heirs, the title became extinct. On his funeral day, local people stood in pouring rain with a sense of disbelief.

Said Dr Perowe (Bishop of Bradford): "Lord Ribblesdale was a friend of two sovereigns, but he is known here best as a friend of all in Gisburn." Not a close friend, mind you, but a man who had a special regard for his family estate.

What manner of man was the last of the line, a contemporary

of the oldest among us? Thomas Lister was French by birth, born at Fontainebleau, where his family were staying. He was brought to Gisburn as a small child and, aged three, was taken South by his footloose parents. He did not return to Gisburn until he was sixteen years old.

Harrow-educated, Thomas was serving in the Army when, on the death of his father, he assumed the title. When he left the Army in 1886, with the rank of Major, he was 32 years of age. Taking his place in the House of Lords as a Liberal, he supported Gladstone until that worthy managed to lose the support of many of the "stately homes of England" with his handling of the Home Rule issue. Ribblesdale became a Liberal Unionist, but returned to the main Liberal fold in 1892 when Gladstone was once again in power and he became a Member of the Privy Council.

At Gisburn, he is best remembered as country squire and sportsman. He loved the archaic terms which clung to the pursuit of deer. He was keen to distance himself from the unsightly spread of industrialisation. Gladstone, who also did not like change, offered him the post of Master of the Queen's Buckhounds, which meant that on the first day of Ascot, Lord Ribblesdale, then living at Englemere House, Ascot, exercised his special privilege of donning the dark green coat and mounting his chestnut horse, to lead the Royal procession down the course.

The squire of Gisburn was married twice. Charlotte, a daughter of Sir Charles Tennant, provided him with five children and died in 1911. During the Boer War, Lord and Lady Ribblesdale sailed to South Africa to be near their elder son, who was in the Army. Lord Ribblesdale faced an angry Boer with nothing more than an umbrella and was so fond of his stocky pony he had it shipped back to England, where it spent the rest of its life in the park at Gisburn.

Ribblesdale's last years were clouded with sorrow. His son Thomas (born in 1878) was killed in action in Somaliland in 1904. The younger son, Charles Alfred, when an undergraduate, was attracted to the political preaching of Keir Hardie and his sympathies lay with the Left. Yet he enlisted in time of war. His body was one of thousands which lay on the beaches of Gallipoli in 1915.

Lord Ribblesdale loved the company of ordinary people and might be seen striding down the main street at Gisburn in the days when cattle fairs were held there. He felled a drover with a single blow because the man had been unmercifully beating a cow with a stick.

One who knew him told me: "Gisburne Park was not particularly well furnished—but it was furnished. They built a special extension for Lord Ribblesdale. He'd had a hunting accident and broke his leg so badly he had to have a steel plate put in it. He couldn't go up and down stairs." Major Yorke says: "The injury to his leg meant he could never wear a hunting boot. He wore strapped-down black trousers under his boot."

In 1919, shortly after the war, Lord Ribblesdale re-married, his bride this time being Ava Willings of Philadelphia, the attractive widow of Col John Jacob Astor, who drowned when the *Titanic* hit an iceberg during its maiden voyage to New York.

A quarter of a century ago, I chatted with Henry Slater, a native of Gisburn who had six hunting seasons with Lord Ribblesdale at Badminton and then worked at Home Farm, Gisburn. Henry recalled his tall, lean figure and the long nose. He was a superb horseman and after one hunt his wife said: "You rode like an intoxicated flea."

The staff at the hall totalled seventeen, and many of them were paid half a crown a week. John Coutts, the butler, distrusted the new telephone—the first in the village—and if it rang during the owner's absence, Coutts (suspecting a call from his Lordship) would straighten his collar and tie before picking up the earphone.

Charles Starkie, the down-to-earth agent, had started work as a labourer and served the estate for forty years. One day, while riding with Ribblesdale, a farm labourer hailed them with "Lordy—t'slates are coming off our barn." Enraged at such an approach, Starkie retorted: "Then climb on to the roof and hold 'em down; you're big enough!"

A villager recalls Lord Ribblesdale's later days, and especially "all the fuss and palaver when he arrived at church." The door was opened for him and he was escorted to the family pew.

In 1925, William Saunders was one of the bearers at the funeral of Lord Ribblesdale. He died in London; the body was conveyed to Hellifield by train and two teams of bearers—one of estate men and the other of tenant farmers—bore it to Gisburn. The coffin, swaddled in the Union Jack, was moved from Gisburne Park to the Church on a horse-drawn, four-wheeled estate cart. William Saunders, then aged twelve, was one of the youngest members of the choir. He has a photograph showing choir and clergy processing round the end of Gisburn Church on their way to the family vault.

Miss Beatrix and Miss Adelaide Lister, the sisters of Lord Ribblesdale, occupied Gisburne Park until their deaths in the 1940s and were known among the staff as "Miss Lister and Miss Adde." Each was an "Honourable". Each had the Lister characteristic of being tall and lean.

"They were very stately and, in the eyes of the village folk, terribly old-fashioned, wearing long dresses. Each carried an umbrella, whatever the weather. They were treated with such enormous respect that whenever they entered a shop, the attendants stood smartly to attention." The two ladies usually summered at Gisburne Park, travelling from their London home with two of their servants. "There was always a cook and a sort of ladies' maid."

In about 1937, William Saunders visited Gisburne Park for the grocery orders. "One day the cook said to me: 'Miss Lister wants to see you before you get paid'. I was taken to her. She stood there, in her old-fashioned clothes, and looked at the account through a monacle. I don't think she checked the figures, but she said: 'Cook's been very extravagant. I'll have to have a word with her'. Then she rang a brass bell and one of the maids escorted me back to the kitchen quarters. The bill was paid."

The Misses Lister were at Gisburn in 1939 and, with the war clouds gathering, they did not return to their South Country home. "During the war, and until they died, I don't think anything at Gisburne Park was altered." They were, of course, regular church-goers, occupying the Lister pew. Henry Slater drove them to worship in an old Austin. The favourite outing of the two ladies was to be driven by Henry on a circuit taking in Barden Tower, in Wharfedale.

When Miss Adelaide Lister, the younger sister, "passed away", she was cremated according to her wishes, having asserted that she was not going to be laid in the dark, dank family tomb at the church. A villager recalls: "That was the first time I had known of anybody round here being cremated. The job had to be done at Blackpool."

Miss Beatrix made it known that, on her death, the family Bible should be handed over to Gisburn Church. William Saunders was the intermediary. "I brought it home and had a jolly good look at it before I gave it to the vicar. It was dated 1613. The wooden backs of the book had crumbled through age.''

In 1943, Gisburne Park was bought by the Hindleys, a manufacturing family from Nelson. This Grade 1 listed building retains the original Georgian splendour both inside and out. Conversion into a private hospital began in early 1984. It is one of the newest and finest in the region.

Bolton-by-Bowland

This is about the prettiest village in Ribblesdale. It
rests at the northerly end of a beautiful amphitheatre
formed by one of those graceful curves of the Ribble.

*William T Palmer, Wanderings
in Ribblesdale (1951).*

IT IS not just the Church, with its high soaring tower, which
evokes the spirit of ancient times. Bolton-by-Bowland has long
been an estate village. The squires of the past did not permit
any unseemly developments.

The magic of Bolton was evident on a sunny day when I led
a party of deer-watchers on a country walk. As we returned in
the late afternoon, our pace quickened in response to lively
music at a fete being held on the School Green.

Venerable buildings straddled one side of the Green and, by
the road, a row of mature chestnuts was in carnival mood, the
trees holding out arms full of multi-tinted leaves. Beyond rose
the battlemented church tower, which—some say—is reminis-
cent of the architecture of Somerset.

The most daring historian implies that the church was being
restored in the fifteenth century with the active interest of an
English king, Henry VI, who had taken sanctuary here after the
ignominious defeat at the Battle of Hexham in May, 1646.

43

Henry was known to be keen on architecture and also to have a love of Somerset.

He would have little peace at Bolton Hall, for Sir Ralph Pudsay had filled it with his family—successively three wives and twenty-five children—as well as with servants. The days must have been punctuated by the squawking of infants.

Rainsber Scar, a feature on Pudsey land where the river curves just inside the gorge, became known as Pudsay's Leap after Sir William Pudsay, astride a horse, leapt down this limestone cliff to escape from the attentions of the law. Pudsay, who had silver mines near Rimington, had broken the law, using his own silver to counterfeit the national coinage.

Pudsay shillings, bearing the escallop, are not easily distinguished from official shillings, for obvious reasons. Pudsay not only survived the descent of Rainsber Scar but managed to get an interview with, and was pardoned by, Queen Elizabeth I, who years before, Pudsay had attended as a page.

James Wilkinson, a fount of local knowledge, was born at the *Coach and Horses,* an inn taken over by his Grandfather, James Wilkinson, in 1880, and continued by his son, John William, until his death in 1942. John's family consisted of two sons and three daughters. The Wilkinson link with the *Coach and Horses* was snapped in 1948.

James remembers when the inn was a social centre, in the sense that anyone who liked a drink and who lived within walking distance joined the village "characters" here on a Saturday night. "There were part drovers about in those days. They usually had a thirst."

Mr Wilkinson said his mother "used to dread the day of the hiring fair, which was on June 28th. Farmers bargained with the Irishmen. Several stalls were erected, selling all manner of goods, including rakes, forks and scythes, which were needed

Bolton-by-Bowland.

at haytime. The place was alive with folk." An Irishman might be hired for £8 a month. "If they got the hay undercover in a fortnight—they were away!"

A break in the haytime routine came when the Irishmen went to church, thence to the nearest pub. "When we were kids, we'd go to *Copy Nook,* where the Irishmen went for their beer. The *Coach and Horses* at Bolton had only a six-day licence. We watched them come out of the pub. There were odd bits o' trouble."

Jock McKinley, a drover from Gisburn auction mart, became drunk and was apprehended by the local policeman. At the Court House in Bolton-by-Bowland, the presiding magistrate, Major Marmaduke Nesfield Wright, the owner of the Bolton estate, said: "Case dismissed. He's suffered enough."

Major Wright, though a small man, was "a real country gentleman, with a deer stalker, tweeds, red waistcoat and long sideboards." His father, C B E Wright, the builder up of the family fortune through coal-mining interests in the Doncaster area, bought the estate from Mrs May Littledale in 1866. Mr Wright immediately had the house enlarged. He also extended the garden and created an underground palm house which was reached by way of a subterranean passage lit by acetylene gas. In the garden were heated greenhouses.

The squire steadfastly refused to allow the railway to pass through Bolton Park. He was "horse mad" and in 1894 the stables held about seventy horses, who were attended by twenty-three grooms. Mr Wright drove a four-in-hand, with two grooms occupying the back seats. Once, when horses pulling a carriage ran away, one wanted to go down Hellifield road and one wanted to go down the village. I heard from a villager that "they finished up at the butcher's shop corner."

Richard Milne-Redhead recalled the days of his youth, early this century, when the staff at Bolton Hall numbered almost a hundred. Mrs Wright (Edith de Cardonnell), who died in 1912, was an invalid who had a donkey-hauled carriage and an attendant groom when she wanted to visit the village or be transported to church.

My own father, as a lad before the 1914-18 War, joined the cricket team from Bradley, near Skipton, on an outing by horse-drawn coach to Bolton-by-Bowland, where a match was played on a ground before the hall. Afterwards, tea was served at a house near the Green.

Godfrey, the elder son of the Wrights, had been killed in action during the Boer War, so that when C B E Wright died in the 1920s, Major Wright and his wife moved into the hall. And when *he* died, the coffin was conveyed from Bolton Hall through the park to the road on a horse-drawn cart, here to be transferred to a hearse. The interment was at Barrow.

The Major was a man who liked a routine. James Wilkinson recalls: "You could nearly set the clock by him when he was on his morning walk with stick and bull terrier (succeeded by a Great Dane). He was especially fond of the Hellifield road. He liked a joke. In his day, the *Coach and Horses* was the venue twice a year of a rent dinner for the farmers and, at another time, tea for the cottagers.

"In spring, there was lamb on the menu and at the back-end dinner, Martinmas, goose was served. If any of the men had any money left after they had paid the rent, they used to stay on for drink and tale-telling. A cottage in the village over half a century ago would be let out at three shillings a week."

Bolton School was attended by farm children, some of whom covered several miles on foot, to school and home again, each day. They carried some lunch and the school had a kettle for boiling up water for a hot mid-day drink.

The Ribble Valley, with its park-like fields, woods and copses, has a sense of mystery when dusk falls on an autumn evening and a shrill scream, mellowed by distance into a whistle, testifies to the presence of a sika stag. The adjacent estates of Gisburne Park and Bolton Hall still hold some of the descendants of deer introduced by Lord Ribblesdale and the Ormerod brothers, of Wyresdale, early this century, with the object of providing sport for the Ribblesdale Buckhounds.

Black fallow were introduced but were not lively enough for the hounds. Tony Jackson recalls meeting a retired gamekeeper, some ten years ago, who clearly recalled when he went with his father to the railway station at Chatburn to collect some deer which had been shipped from Ireland into Liverpool and then transported by train to Chatburn, to be emparked in the Gisburn area. These sika deer, for such they were, presumably came from Powerscourt, south of Dublin, where the breed had been introduced about 1860.

The Buckhounds are recalled by Major Yorke as being like large foxhounds. "Eventually they had what they called a Kerry Beagle, large and dark tan, more like a bloodhound, with a tremendous voice. You could hear the pack half a mile away." The Buckhounds had some long runs. "I've got the head of one they ran flat out from Sawley and killed in the river near Halton bridge."

Sika were to become numerous and widespread in the Ribble Valley, spreading—with the creation of big new conifer forests—to the upper Hodder. When James Wilkinson, as a child, was playing in the beck, a hunted stag passed close by. "It came out of the beck in the village, ran up towards the church, jumped up into the churchyard (there was no fence on top of the wall then) and ran down the fields.   When we went to church, we had to pass Church Gates, then the home of Mr Macalpine, Master of the Hunt. If the front door was opened, a mounted deer head was to be seen on the wall."

A man who was born at Bolton Mill in 1914 told me of two bizarre objects in the sale which preceded the demolition of Bolton Hall. "There were two skeletons—one of a man and the other of a horse—and I think they were bought by Stonyhurst College." Richard Milne-Redhead noted that the skeletons of man, horse and dog were kept in the harness room.

When I began a twenty-five year study of the behaviour of sika deer in the Bolton-by-Bowland area, the landscape had a raggedness which went as a vast acreage of old pasture was ploughed and re-seeded with a sappy ryegrass mix for silage-making.

Continued on page 57.

Collection of James Wilkinson.

LORD RIBBLESDALE, KNOWN AS "THE ARISTOCRAT", AT
A GISBURN MEET NOT LONG BEFORE HIS DEATH IN 1925.

Above: The great days at Bolton Hall, from a photograph by E. Buck of Clitheroe.
Below: Browsholme Hall, historic home of the Parker family, who were Bow-bearers in Bowland Forest.

Right: Sika stag in velvet.
Below: Blocked-in entry for deer in a building on the Gisburn Estate which has been demolished.

Left: A handsome cairn, made by Clitheroe Scouts on Pendle Hill. Nearby is a much appreciated windbreak, complete with stone seats.

Below: The Pudsay tomb in Bolton-by-Bowland Church. This famous old family provided hospitality for a fugitive King in the fifteenth century.

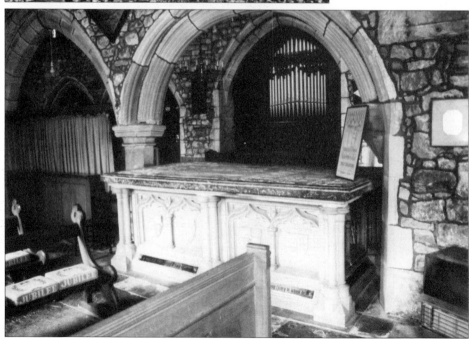

Above: Lily pond in the grounds of Stonyhurst College, which is run by the Jesuits.
Right: Tower of New-church-in-Pendle. Notice the oval feature with a dark mark, said to represent the all-seeing house of God.

Opposite page: Detail of the Whalley Abbey stonework and a view of finely-carved woodwork in the parish church.

Above: Crest of the Parkers of Browsholme.

Right: Carving of an angel at Whalley Abbey.

Right: Canalising the Ribble near Cow Bridge.
Below: Morris Dancers at Gisburn.
Bottom: The picture postcard village of Downham.

Hay-making had previously been the rule, the fields—always so herby—being mown with a variety of primitive attachments to tractors until progress brought the flail-mowers. Big-bag silage is now a general practise. The sun brings a gleam to rows of large plastic bags which are stored out of doors. The old out-barns are crumbling or being converted into other uses.

The first of my farmer friends on the deer range was Jimmy Dinsdale, of Monubent Head. Soon I had got to know the neighbouring farmers, and in particular Arthur Hodgson of New Ing. When I was not watching deer, I could observe brown hares by the dozen. I counted forty feeding in one large field as it began to green-up after the winter. When a hare shoot was planned, the bag was invariably over a hundred.

When the "night shift" of the wild came on duty, I heard three grunts and a squeak, drawing my attention to the ter-ritorial flight of a woodcock—a podgy bird, maintaining an elevation of about fifty feet, calling at regular intervals. The Ribble Valley, with its dry open woods, is ideal for woodcock.

Many years ago, it was a joy to visit the rock garden which Richard Milne-Redhead, a Mancunian, founded at Holden, near Bolton-by-Bowland. He bought Holden Clough in January, 1877, the sale price including the remains of two lead mines and also a "prolific trout stream". Immediately, he set to work on a rock garden, which then was a novel idea.

His enthusiasm for plants actually began in the 1850s. Richard visited the Holy Land and wrote a book about the Palestinian flora, though no publisher was found. His grand-son, also named Richard, told me the stone was taken from a local beck. "It was quite a mixture—limestone, gritstone and the calliards which could not be broken up, even with a sledge-hammer."

Grandfather had been a great traveller, visiting Brazil and the

West Indies. He knew Europe and Russia well. He also had a sojourn in India. He did not collect plants systematically or as obsessively as did the more famous Reginald Farrer, of Clapham, who became widely known for his interest in rock gardens.

Richard's son, Arthur Cecil Milne-Redhead, also had a love of botany. At Holden he made a water garden and planted up the grass tennis court with conifers. The Milne-Redheads had a mutual interest in gardening with the Farrers. The Richard I knew—he was Arthur's second son—recalled his young days when he cycled from Holden to Clapham, there to look round Reginald Farrer's famous rock garden and to watch George Redman attending to the nursery in the frequent absence, through overseas travels, of Reginald himself.

Farrer devised rock gardens in which the rock was positioned to resemble a natural run of strata. At Holden Clough, in those pioneering days, there was no such pretension. "The stones were put in higgledy-piggledy," Richard Milne-Redhead told me.

The Milne-Redheads (who were Tory) did not mix socially with the Farrers (who then were Liberals). "Different political persuasions did make for social distinctions in those days." Reginald Farrer—"a stocky man, brisk in his speech and averse to wasting time"—was an occasional visitor to Holden Clough where once, emotionally overcome by the beauty of a particular alpine plant, he prostrated himself before it and then rolled on the ground in ecstacy.

Sawley and the Abbey

Sawley Brow, on the Gisburn road, was hated as a
trap for boastful drivers, for low-powered cars and
for ultra-big luxury models as well.

William T Palmer (1951).

IN THE old days, Sawley was best-known to the motoring
fraternity for its wicked combination of gradient, narrowness
and frequent bends. Early this century, it was classified in the
Contour Book as II, with the comment: "Pretty hilly from
Sawley to Gisburn."

Fred Ellis, of Settle, who had some entertaining experiences
of early motoring days to relate, once told me he was driving
up Sawley Brow in a Model T Ford when the engine cut. He
had to think quickly for on that type of car the foot-brake was
satisfactory but the hand-brake soon wore out. "So I was
stuck, holding the car with the foot-brake but not being able to
get out. Yet I had to get out and put in some petrol."

His solution was to grab a jack which was carried in the back
and, with deft foot movements, slipped from the driving sweat
and put the jack under a back wheel before the car could run
away. Fred then drove the car on to some level ground—and
walked back to pick up the jack.

Whenever there was a sprinkling of snow, and an articulated vehicle jack-knifed, Sawley Brow made headline news. In the holiday season, this Gisburn road was a busy route leading to Blackpool, an accident or a breakdown at Sawley leading to frayed nerves. A motorist could command attention at a social gathering by remarking: "And do you know, I had a flat tyre on Sawley Brow".

Part of the old road may be seen from those who drive up the hill from Sawley to the multi-laned highway in use today. All the traffic once poured through Sawley itself, where a welcome was provided by the (now much extended) *Spread Eagle.*

A monastic arch, extending half way across the road, accommodated eastbound traffic. The central part of the road was occupied by a broad grass verge sprouting road signs, reflectors and large pieces of dressed stone which were formerly part of the abbey. The arch was dismantled, to be re-built at the gateway to a field—surely the most impressive field gateway in the country.

The few remains of Sawley Abbey are "open to view" at no charge. The material used by the monks was shaly and crumbly; at the Dissolution (1536) the best stone was re-cycled by being incorporated in new buildings elsewhere. Salley (as it was originally called) was a Cistercian abbey, daughter of Fountains, founded in 1147 and always struggling to survive, especially when, 160 years later, Whalley Abbey was founded on a site that proved to be uncomfortably close.

The Sawley monks had complained about the weather, which was dull and wet. Corn developed well but the ears were inclined to rot on the stalk. A submission to the Pope, following the "depredation and burning" of Salley by the Scots in the fourteen century, described the place as being "in the most castaway and remote parts of all our kingdom, towards Irish Sea, and moreover in a country wonderfully woody and hilly and, on account of the too great frequency of storms, for the most part barren and unfruitful.''

With the Cistercians of Whalley intercepting fish before they could reach Sawley, there was a cause for more discontent, the salmon being ''dearer when they do come by a third of a penny.'' No one sought fish with rod and line (angling as such was not practised until the fifteenth century). The monks trapped and netted the salmon and sea trout on their spawning run. They had ingenious traps for eels.

Monastic gateway (now a field gate!) at Sawley.

Chatburn Village

St Ceadda's shady stream.

T D Whitaker, History of Whalley.

THE Clitheroe by-pass is set on a dry limestone ridge, being (roughly) on the line of the Roman road from Ribchester to Ilkley. Today, the traffic passes with a whine and a whoosh. It is tempting to think of earlier travellers—right back to the days of the "gold" road: a track (for it must have been little more than this) used by early folk who had trading links with Ireland.

Men of the Bronze Age were probably the first to use this "ancient trackway", intent on acquiring the gold, tin and other metals from Ireland. They returned to the mouth of the Ribble, thence across what is now Yorkshire to the coast at a point just south of the chalk cliffs. This 112-mile long route (including the navigable stretch of Ribble) used the Aire Gap as a low-level way through the Pennines.

The much later Roman connection with the limestone ridge near Chatburn was proved when a large hoard of coins was found between the village and Worston, where the map indicates the line of the road which provided a swift connection between Chester and York. Clitheroe's modern by-pass also

Chatburn.

by-passes Chatburn and relegates to second place the "new" road from Clitheroe, which had been opened in 1826.

Chatburn is associated in popular imagination with another great traveller, Chad, one of the Celtic missionaries who were surely much tougher characters than is suggested by the haloed imagies on stained glass in Victorian churches. Those who re-Christianised the North after the Dark Ages included itinerant preachers who trudged along tracks through the forests and spoke out-of-doors.

There is a common belief that the placename Chatburn relates to St Chad. Harold Woods, who takes an interest in the history of his native place, told me that two former Head-masters of Chatburn C of E School—Messrs Waite (1875-1920) and Aldersley (1920-1953) taught that the village was named after the Celtic "coed", meaning a wood by the stream.

A watercourse named Heys Brook on the Ordnance Survey has its source on the Big End of Pendle and is a tributary of the Ribble. If the link between Chad and Chatburn had been strong, then surely the church, which dates from early last century, would have been dedicated to him. It wasn't.

Many writers overlook St Martin's association with Chatburn. A Hermitage of Chatburn, with land and meadow, dedicated to St Martin, were granted by John o'Gaunt, Duke of Lancaster, to Brother Robert de Goldbourne in 1372. In the first half of the sixteenth century, a chapel is said to have been dedicated to him. St Martin features in stained glass in Christ Church, along with St Paulinus, who is said to have been the first missionary to enter the Ribble Valley. You will look in vain for a window featuring Chad.

Chatburn, a small community which evolved in Norman times, was first mentioned in 1241. For centuries, life was quiet if not tranquil. Then Chatburn became yet another village near the textile belt of East Lancashire to acquire a mill.

Each morning, the villagers were roused early by the clatter of clogs on stone as the workers went to the mill, a woman wearing the traditional Paisley shawl. Within living memory, the clogs were made (and repaired) by Charles Isherwood. Mr Woods told me that the wearing of clogs and shawls by older women seems to have gradually declined in the late 1930s and 1940s. Scarcely any were to be seen after the 1939-45 war.

An early cotton mill, belonging to the Hargreaves family, was in production in 1859. (Christ Church, having been consecrated in 1838, was enlarged in 1881, presumably because the local mill had drawn in a large number of workers). A serious fire occurred in 1905. In the following year, a new owner, Harry Broughton, was in buoyant mood and increased the number of Lancashire looms from 312 to 1,000 by 1926.

There were now four weaving sheds, in which a wide variety of coloured goods was produced. The brisk trade led the owner (in 1920) to build a new warehouse and circular brick chimney with a height of 150 ft. The smoke from the Lancashire boilers to the chimney was carried through a tunnel (passing under the road).

Between 1909 and 1920, Broughton Bros., the mill-owners, constructed about one hundred brick houses, set in terraces, and available to the workers for rent. When the mill was sold to Smith and Nephew, Broughtons offered the tenants the opportunity of buying their houses. Many a fine dwelling exchanged hands at between £1,100 and £1,300 (and are now worth between £40,000 and £60,000). The mill was closed in July, 1991, and subsequently demolished, the site being developed for even more houses.

Chatburn is built on solid limestone. The second industry was quarrying, the largest enterprise being Bold Venture (opened in 1836 and greatly extended in 1850 on the arrival of the Bolton, Blackburn, Clitheroe and West Yorkshire Railway). Here were three large kilns and a private rail siding to distribute the lime.

Chatburn.

After the 1939-45 war, the enterprise was taken over by Ribblesdale Cement Company. At the time of my visit, there was considerable local concern about proposals for deep-quarrying. After fifty years of noise and dust, the quarry would be allowed to fill with water.

Chatburn had its brief wartime blitz. At about 2 p.m., on October 30, 1940, bombs from a single German bomber caused extensive structural damage to shops and buildings in the centre of the village. Mill roofs and glass windows were shattered. Several villagers died, among them Miss Alice Robinson whose home received a direct hit; she lingered for a few days but died in hospital. Miss Robinson's love of Chatburn is remembered. She left a substantial sum of money to provide the village with playing fields.

The bomb which demolished her home also killed the driver of a petrol tanker which was passing near the house on its way through Chatburn. A man and woman living nearby died of shock.

Clitheroe station is being refurbished for the return of passenger services from Clitheroe to Blackburn. Chatburn stood on what became the Lancashire and Yorkshire Railway (Lanky), which in 1880 pushed a line through to Hellifield. The original proposal, to connect with Long Preston, was—as related—blocked by Mr Wright of Bolton Hall.

Harold Woods began railway work at Chatburn in 1929, when there was a staff of 23 people for this area alone.

Chatburn station was closed on September 1, 1962.

Bonnie Downham

When Downham stones with diamonds rank
And cockles be with pearls compared
When gold is made of grey goose wings
Then shall I and my love be married.

Anon, A Balade of Maryage (17th century).

THE road from Chatburn has its moment of glory when crossing the high bridge over the Clitheroe by-pass. It then enters a stretch shaded by the walls and trees at the edge of the Downham Hall parkland.

A large stone near the entrance to the Hall is said to mark the final resting place of two Roman legionnaires who died at the hands of the Brigantes. It is a pretty tale, as is another story (told to me by Jim Fishwick, of happy memory) that the stone turns several times at midnight when it hears the church bells. (This never happens, of course, a stone having no ears).

Where the road from Chatburn breaks into full sunlight, the dream village of Downham is in view, and beyond is t'Big End o' Pendle. The village is written up in a local guide book in justifiably glowing terms. Downham "nestles under the bulk of Pendle" and is "one of the loveliest villages in Lancashire". The brook "gurgles". The "gnarled" old sycamore spreads its branches over the preserved village stocks.

The *George and Dragon* inn was re-named *The Assheton Arms*, having the coat of arms of the illustrous local family (residents at Downham for over four hundred years) painted on the name board. The post office is also a tourist information centre and cafe.

Down the hill, a duck-infested beck ripples near old cottages, some of them, in Chapel Brow, being formerly associated with handloom weavers. Downham has its grander buildings, mini-halls in the vernacular style of architecture. This pretty Lancashire village is devoid of yellow roadside lines, overhead telephone wires, signs and television aerials, apart from the communal aerial on the hill behind the inn.

Just over thirty years ago, *Whistle Down the Wind* was filmed in this area. It has been used for scenes from a production of *Wuthering Heights.* A local man observes: "We've kept Downham unspoilt. So the film people don't have much to do if they're 'shooting' scenes about the old days."

Downham Hall is the home of Lord Clitheroe, whose family (the Asshetons) have lived here for over four centuries. The middle part of the hall dates back to the twelfth century. A lady born in the village proudly recalls being among the spectators in the grounds in 1938 when Queen Mary visited the hall. The estate takes in the old manor of Downham, including a good deal of Pendle Hill, and is bounded by Worston, Chatburn and Rimington.

Downham Church, perched on the hillside, is packed with memorials to the Asshetons, whose family surname is derived from Ashton-under-Lyne, where they settled soon after the Norman Conquest. The Assheton Sermon is preached here on January 29th, being the anniversary of the death of Sir Ralph Assheton, Lord of the Manor, Member of Parliament for Clitheroe in the Long Parliament, an active supporter of the

68

Parliamentary cause in the Civil War and High Sheriff of Lancashire.

In 1940, the Sermon was not preached until February, having been postponed for the first time in 260 years because of inclement weather. And in 1994, the event was held earlier in the month so that an American parson, the Rev Pat Houston from North Carolina, who had been in Downham for a year on an exchange visit, could have the honour of preaching before flying back to the New World.

The local fell race once began at the Church and took in the Big End of Pendle, following which the runners could be seen breaking the skyline on the Hill before they descended to the village. Now, with so many competitors (some of whom are over seventy years old) and visitors, the race begins at the bottom end of the village. The strongest runners complete the circuit in about 43 minutes. The junior race takes in Worsaw Hill, one of the Ribble Valley "reef knolls".

On sunny days, there is a responsive gleam from the roofs of scores of cars. A new car park has been made, in one corner of which stood a redundant shippon, complete with booses, divisions between the stalls. The building was transformed into a toilet block—a toilet block which won a national award for the excellence of the design. This impressive block has facilities for Ladies and Gents, plus a changing room for visitors with babies. There is also an up-to-date information board on which details of local events are displayed.

Clitheroe

Never will I forget the beauty of the mist-shrouded
valley as we saw it from Pendle—after a night on the
summit—when the only visible features were the two
detached rocks, the castle, the church and Clitheroe
veiled between.

Jessica Lofthouse, in "Clitheroe
800 Years", 1986.

ITS origins go back to the proverbial "mists of antiquity" but
it is convenient to date the genesis of Clitheroe from the twelfth
century, when Roger de Poitou—among the new-rich following
the Norman Conquest—received a grant of land. Robert de
Lacy, Lord of the Honour of Clitheroe, built the castle on a
limestone knoll.

As castles go, this was relatively small. It does have that
prime requirement—a commanding position. A stroller along
Castle Street at Clitheroe has his or her attention drawn, again
and again, to the sturdy keep.

The de Lacys were anxious to have a secure base, an ever-
present reminder, to the native folk, of Norman might and a
centre from which to administer a large area. They took out
divine insurance cover through being generous to the Church.
A chapel dedicated to St Michael stood within the castle walls.

A knoll along the limestone ridge was the ideal setting for a church which was mentioned as early as 1122, when a local lord, Hugh de Laval, granted it to the Priory of St John in Pontefract. Clitheroe evolved as a huddle of buildings between Castle and Church.

Clitheroe is derived from *Cled-dwr*, a British word, meaning hill or rock by the water, presumably the Ribble—though Clitheroe has its own little watercourse and three old town wells. Water is the first requirement of a settlement. The town's motto emphasises this, being: "The rock will remain and the river will flow."

The second main requirement is land on which to grow food-crops. Clitheroe, at the heart of the bountiful Ribble Valley, had land and to spare. The hamlet became a village; the village grew to a town, becoming the second oldest borough in Lancashire (the oldest, for the record, is Wigan). Clitheroe Royal Grammar School was founded in 1554 (on a site in the parish churchyard). Girls were admitted in 1915 and now they have their own Grammar School in Chatburn Road.

As the old town waxed, the castle waned. It was slighted in Cromwellian times, though the hole in the east wall of the Keep is said to have been caused when the devil threw a rock from Pendle Hill. In an early drawing of the castle, an artist added a few windows for effect!

Today, the remains of the Keep have been consolidated. The substantial building used by the Steward for the Honour of Clitheroe is a Museum, one of the largest exhibits being the restored ferryboat which transported people across the river at Hacking. The Museum evokes, through sound effects, life as it was in an Edwardian kitchen and also reminds us of an early printing press and clogger's workshop.

Also on Castle Hill is the old Court House (for the recovery of debts under forty shillings) and later used by the Steward. Today, the building is a modern Tower of Babel, being full of taped voices—the 85,000 recordings of The North West Sound Archive. Row after row of taped memories of local life, industry and tradition evoke local life through the words of those who experienced it.

You will look in vain on the second of Clitheroe's limestone knolls for traces of the church of eight hundred years ago; the present church dates from 1828. The spire, added to the tower in the 1840s, emulated that at Chesterfield and became twisted. The tidy Clitheronians arranged, in 1969, for it to be straightened.

On my very first visit to Clitheroe, someone urged me to be cautious when mentioning local people, adding: "Kick a man at the top of Castle Street, and by the time you've walked to the bottom you'll see five other men rubbing their shins!" There are close relationships, though Clitheroe is increasingly a dormitory town for Blackburn, Burnley and even Manchester. This is reflected in house prices. A terrace house is valued at about £65,000.

Clitheroe became partly industrialised but never lost its market town appeal nor become part of an East Lancashire conurbation. The country comes to town on market day. For years, livestock was offered for sale in the main street, which was unsanitary and, periodically, exciting when a beast ran amock. The old cattle market was closed on the transfer of its business to a range of new buildings on the Salthill Industrial Estate (known to local people as "Up t'Brooks).

Salthill offers the humbling experience of a geological trail, having exposures of limestone, rich in fossils from the time when this area was somewhere near the Equator and covered by a warm sea, with colourful reefs and a variety of primitive life-forms. The Continental drift theory accounts for its present position.

Thirty years ago, when seeking information about Clitheroe, I was astonished to discover there was no Town Hall as such. The Surveyor worked in what had been the local Masonic temple in Church Street. The Public Health Office, though in the same general warren of small rooms, was entered from York Street.

The Treasurer's suite of offices lay in a former private house in Church Street and the Town Clerk presided over offices in a building near the Castle Keep—or what remained of the Castle Keep: just enough to create a blunt but powerful image when viewed from Castle Street.

Now there is a Town Council and a Mayor-making, with a parade of civic dignitaries. The Ribble Valley Borough Council sprang into existence when the Boundary Commission changed the old boundaries in 1974. In the Clitheroe of early 1994, there is further talk of local government re-organisation.

Three decades ago, the main street, on the ridge of a hill, with streets sloping down on either side, was taking all the traffic on the A.59. A vehicle count on a July Tuesday in 1960, between 2 p.m. and 10 p.m., revealed that 1,138 entered the town from Chatburn and 1,140 went out at the other side, giving a difference of only two. Today, a one-way traffic system applies. The "through" traffic passes, with a whine and whoosh, on a by-pass which might be an engineering triumph but lacerated a once pleasant part of the valley.

Quarrying interests account for a modernistic skyline between Clitheroe and Chatburn. In the old days, it was King Cotton's huge mills and lofty chimneys which transformed the town. John Parker built the first local spinning mill at Low Moor in 1782. The demand for workers for this and several other cotton mills which were in existence by 1848, led to the employment of inmates from London hospitals and also child labour.

The Low Moor enterprise reached a gigantic size. So did Primrose Mill, founded by James Thomson, built for almost a thousand spindles and later equipped with Lancashire looms. This enterprise did not long survive Thomson's death. Some of the redundant workers emigrated to America. The premises were so large that they were eventually taken up by three concerns, one of them concerned with calico printing.

At Clitheroe, in the nineteen-nineties, Trutex devote themselves to garments. The industrial "heavies" are Castle Cement and ICI. The chimney of the former tickles the clouds and emits white smoke which the Ribble Valley folk consult each morning when assessing the weather conditions. Which way is the smoke blowing? Is it rising or extending horizontally, with a stiff wind behind it? Lofty installations, illuminated at night, give a space-age appearance to the valley.

Limestone, the bedrock of the Ribble Valley has, since medieval days, been closely associated with the Clitheroe area. The products were transported in panniers by Lime Gals—pack ponies, of a type bred in Galloway, which delivered limestone to the industrial and coastal areas. They are said to have returned to Clitheroe with loads of shellfish from Morecambe Bay. It is recorded that Lime Gals carried between 500 and 1,000 loads a day (so there must have been other products besides shellfish on the return journey). With the arrival of the railway early last century, the Lime Gals became redundant.

It was not until the early part of this century that cement production was established, using the old type vertical kilns, the lime being marketed using the brand name "Isis Cement". The quarry was closed down by the owners, the Spackman family, in 1926.

Almost ten years were to pass before Tunnel Cement Ltd and Ketton Portland Cement Co., Ltd., became interested in re-establishing cement production in the area. They joined forces and established Ribblesdale Cement, Ltd. Following successful site trials and the purchase of the Horrocksford Hall Farm Estate, they built the first production unit in 1935. This lit up in November, 1936, and other kilns were added.

All the units were of the "wet" process type (so called because water was used to make a slurry, acting as a conveying agent to a kiln. This was energy intensive, the water having to be dried off immediately the slurry entered the kiln before the production of cement clinker could begin. In 1983, a £30 million "dry" process unit came into production, considerably reduction coal consumption and employing other cost-cutting technology.

The name "Castle Cement" and the appearance of the red turret as a trademark appeared in 1984. Since 1988, the enterprise has been under Norwegian ownership. Cement is marketed across the northern half of England and in southern Scotland, being mainly transported as "loose" cement in bulk tankers. Forty per cent of sales are in Lancashire and Greater Manchester.

Many people are uneasy about proposals to extend Bellman Quarry over a period of fifty years. Nature has been doing its best to cover old wounds to the landscape and Bellman's is a valuable nature reserve, having been designated as a Site of Special Scientific Interest.

Waddington Ways

One of the Ribble Valley's best known villages, the
attractive Coronation Gardens appear on many a
postcard and even on biscuit tins.

From a local guide book.

KING HENRY VI, having spent some time as a fugitive at
Bolton-by-Bowland, had a year's residence at Waddington Hall
before being betrayed to the Yorkists in 1465. It is recorded that
he escaped from the Hall by way of a secret panel and staircase
from the dining room. When he reached Brungerley, he was
captured.

This is one of the stirring incidents from the history of a
village which used to be in Yorkshire and featured for some
years among the prize-winners in best-kept village competi-
tions. An area near the church has been attractively landscaped
and appeals to visitors.

The parish church at Waddington is dedicated to St Helen
but those who know it well are inclined to think first of Wadda,
who is pictured in stained glass above the door in the belfry
tower. He was "a blond Anglo-Saxon giant with whiskers and
fierce blue eyes." Wadda is also known as Wade—hence the
name Waddington, Wade's settlement, or so they say.

The stained glass in the church tower was paid for by John Waddington, of Waddington Hall, who claimed to be descended from Wade. The old warrier is said to have lived on what is still known as Wade's Hill, a limestone knoll just across the Ribble from Clitheroe. Here, too, is found Waddow Hall, a mid-nineteenth century mansion, known throughout the land—and in many places abroad—because it belongs to the Girl Guides Association.

I arrived, seeking information, on one of the rare sunny days early in 1994, when snowdrops had appeared, there was a sparkle on the Ribble weir and a woodman was cutting into handy sections the trunk of a 150 year old beech tree, the victim

Waddow Hall.

of a recent gale. As a Guide Training Centre, Waddow Hall maintains a commendable neatness. It has been so since the autumn of 1927, when the Association leased the house and estate, "the site of an Anglo-Saxon Chief's camp".

The Princess Royal officially opened the Centre in the presence of Lady Baden-Powell and 1,500 Guides who, it is recalled, lined the drive on the wettest day of the year. Waddow was purchased in the following year for £9,000. Two years later, Brungerley Farm had become part of the estate. A booklet refers to the buildings having a tranquillity "which is barely touched by the excitement of holidaying Brownies or the energetic pursuits of camping Guides and Rangers."

As I surveyed a well-manicured landscape sweeping down to the Ribble, I was impressed by the recorded history of the place—by the Domesday mention of two carcutes or parcels of the lands of Roger of Poictou" at Wadetun, soon to be acquired by the de Lacys. In the thirteenth century, a branch of the Tempest family began a four hundred year long residence of the village, their generosity in paying for a priest at Waddington being recalled annually when Waddow pays an annual stipend to the vicar—now "all of £1.34p."

The Tempests may have built Waddow Hall as a dower house. The most celebrated resident was not the owner, nor a member of his family, but a serving maid, Peg O'Nell, who fell in love with the eldest son of the family. His mother expressed a wish that Peg would fall and break her neck. The spirited Peg replied that if this happened, she would put a curse on Waddow and, every seventh year, the Ribble would claim a life—not necessarily a human life.

Peg died when she slipped on the ice around a well which now bears her name—Peg O'Nell's Well. Local people, knowing of her curse, were apt to blame her restless spirit if anything went wrong. On 'Peg's Night'—the last night of every seventh year—a life was claimed. Sometimes it was a human life, as in the case of a young horseman, riding from Clitheroe to Waddington. It was his sacrifice that ended Peg's reign of terror.

In those days, no bridge existed at Brungerley; there was just a ford, which could be dangerous at floodtime. The horseman was reckless in wanting to cross with the river in spate. An inn-keeper tried to dissuade him. It was Peg's Night! He simply laughed. If he died, he would see to it that Peg did not worry anyone again. It was the last anyone saw of the man or horse. And the last time Peg proved troublesome.

Wilkinsons, Weddells, Ramsdens and Garnetts were the owners from 1657 until 1928, and the opening of a Girl Guide centre.

Well-Watered Mitton

Hodder, Calder, Ribble and rain
They all meet together in Mitton demesne.

Traditional rhyme.

I HAVE a special love for what I call Shireburn Country—a tract of the Ribble Valley, from Mitton to Stonyhurst, the history of which is dominated by one illustrious family.

Shireburn Country takes in Kemple End and the confluence of the Hodder and Ribble. From a farming point of view it is dog and stick country, though nowadays the farmer and his dog travel by all-terrain vehicle and have an array of powerful machines to help them.

Haytime, once a hand operation, is scarcely known today as grass is ensiled to provide food for the wintering stock. The Shireburns, who died out years ago, would have gasped with amazement to see silage stored in rows of big bags, most of them black, though silvered where they catch the eye of the sun.

If you would see a memorial to the Shireburns (or Sherburnes), then look about you, especially at Stonyhurst, their old home, rising like a palace, with towers and cupolas, beyond a sweep of parkland. Less evident is the connection between the family and the thirteenth century church of All Hallows at Great Mitton—until you enter, to see a splendid Shireburn Chapel.

Mitton Church is a large, well-buttressed edifice of native stone and, within, of ancient oak, forming rafters and screens. Mitton—a name derived from the farm at the "mythe" or junction of two streams—has an an enviable position overlooking river, field and copse.

The finest approach to the hamlet is on foot, walking beside the Ribble from Edisford. Himalayan balsam has run riot and even grows lustily from crevices in a heap of stones. The path passes a farmhouse with the curious name of Fishes and Peggy Hall.

An aqueduct arches itself over the Ribble. From the Mitton flats, the hamlet is seen as a cluster of buildings on a limestone ridge, with the Church tower as the main focal point. The bridge spanning the Ribble replaced a ferry which was in use as late as 1810. The local inn, known as the *Mitton Boat,* was re-named *The Aspinall Arms* in quite recent times.

In the happy days when rural folk did not bother to lock their doors, for no one would dream of stealing anything, Mitton Church could be visited with no more effort than turning the door handle. It is now kept locked, except on Sundays. The key is available locally on demand.

All Hallows was first commended to me by a former incumbent, the Ven F G Ackerley, the author of a booklet about the church, in which he noted that the earliest part is the nave (c1270), the chancel being added some twenty-five years later.

The tower dates from the early fifteenth century, being mentioned in a document dated 1438.

The window popularly known as the Lepers' Window—an idea which was made the subject of the nineteenth century stained glass that fills it—cannot have been used by lepers, who were not allowed to enter a churchyard, much less the church. They had their own place of worship and chaplain at nearby Edisford.

I usually make directly for the Shireburn/Sherburne Chapel, which was built on the site of the chantry of St Nicholas by Sir Richard. He died in 1594, the year of the chapel's completion. Sir Richard was known as old Fiddle of God, from his usual oath, Fidele de Dieu—or Friend of God. Effigies of the family are set for all time in alabaster.

On one tomb are two symbolic figures of children, there being a smiling boy on the left and, on the right, a weeping boy; he sheds an alabaster tear. The tomb is bedecked with emblems of mortality—the skull and crossbones, a scythe and spring flowers, cut off in their prime.

Below the north wall of the Shireburn Chapel lay a figure cut in freestone—an exact replica of an alabaster monument of Sir Richard Sherburne. Ackerley wrote: "Either it was intended to be a copy placed out of doors in addition to the more costly tomb within or it was the original monument, displaced later by Roiley's alabaster work.

"The story that it was made as the result of a bet by a local mason—that he could execute as good a monument as the more expensive one—may be dismissed as mere nonsense."

In 1430, a dispute broke out about the seemingly trivial matter of seats for certain ladies. Even the parson was not able to resolve the squabbling over places at worship. Richard Sherburne gave judgement, naming three ladies who were to "kneel at the head form in Mitton kirk." Others were to kneel "at the forme beneath them." They were all to swear "upon a book upon the Brig of Hoder to p'forme these co'nants on the payne of forfeiting my friendship." The matter was promptly resolved.

At Mitton are bits and pieces of old Ribblesdale abbeys. The church's screen came from Sawley Abbey and (they say) a few stones over the doorway of the *Three Fishes* were brought here from Whalley Abbey.

Three rivers meet in the Mitton area. A good map is needed to clarify the situation. Those who set off confidently along a footpath to the south of the river find themselves on a rapidly narrowing wedge of country until eventually they stand at the confluence of Hodder and Ribble.

Jessica Lofthouse, writing long before the 1974 boundary revision, mentioned a "triangle of Yorkshire thrust into Lancashire."

Parkers at Browsholme

God blesse Edmund Parker and all that with hym wonnes
Hys five daughters and hys seven sons.

Needlework dated 1450.

I FIRST visited Browsholme in 1961, when the Regency rooms of this historic hall, home of the Parker family for 450 years, were being restored by Col R G Parker. Having attended to the fabric of Browsholme during the past seven years, the man whose ancestors were keepers of Bowland Forest and bow-bearers from the days of the first Queen Elizabeth, was tackling the interior with the help of a distinguished architect, Sir Albert Richardson.

When I took a party of members of the British Deer Society to Browsholme, they were fascinated by the deer on the crest of the Parker family—an allusion to the old Forest of Bowland—and by fact that Colonel Parker himself addressed us on the lawn, then personally took us around his historic house.

Browsholme (pronounce it Broos'am) has some sixty rooms, packed with fascinating domestic objects from almost every age of English history, as well as valuable china and paintings.

The name of this prominent Bowland family came from its duties as keepers of the Forest. For six hundred years, the hall and estate descended by way of the male line. The present

84

building was constructed in 1507. The porch, designed by Thomas Holt, of York, about 1595, includes three orders of Greek architecture. Thomas Lister Parker, living here early last century, was a friend of the Prince Regent. Parker spent a fortune on the house. Reputedly, the landscape gardens alone cost over £100,000.

With old Colonel Parker as my guide, I saw a veritable assortment of objects, a Cromwellian long clock standing near an aluminium girder, part of the first Zeppelin to be brought down in England in the 1914-18 war. There was also the stirrup gauge. At one time no dog could be kept in the Forest unless it could pass through a gauge or stirrup, which now hangs near the fireplace. The Parkers had to uphold this law.

Ironically, the last time the small gauge was used (in 1780), John Parker had been elected M.P. for Clitheroe, opposing the nominee of the Duke of Buccleuch, who had the Honour of Clitheroe. So the Duke's ladies, feeling spiteful, insisted that a pack of beagles kept at Browsholme should be tested. They failed to pass and were destroyed.

I heard that Browsholme has its ghost—that of a horse which John Parker, who lived in the latter part of the eighteenth century, in a moment of abandonment, rode up the main staircase, having "a bit of an accident". John recovered; the horse died. Its picture hangs in the Velvet Room. Tradition insists that if the picture falls, one of the Parker family will die.

An object not being shown to the general public at that time was a skull kept in a court cupboard in the hall. The fortunes of Browsholme and of the Parkers are closely bound up with it. The skull, said to have belonged to one of the martyrs of the Pilgrimage of Grace, used to lie in the chapel on the top storey. When this storey was removed, the skull was reverently placed in the cupboard.

In the late 1850s, Edward Parker, then at Harrow, returned home on holiday, found the skull and buried it quietly in the garden. Disaster struck the hall and the family. The facade of the building began to fall away. Fires broke out. Deaths occurred. When the frightened youngster admitted what he had done, the skull was dug up and taken indoors. The run of disaster came to an end.

Among the fascinating structures which were formerly on the Browsholme Estate is Spire, a lofty and thick wall erected by the Parker family as a landmark. It is attached to a farmhouse.

Following the Hodder

A great bed of rushes on the fell top conserves the water and gives birth to the river. From rushes dipping over the peat-hag, water drips unceasingly, dimpling the blackness below. And so Hodder is born.

Jessica Lofthouse, Three Rivers (1946).

NEAR where the Hodder (the "pleasant stream") has its source beyond Stocks Reservoir is the Cross of Greet, now just a name on a map but once a marker at the division of two counties. There is a Scottishness about the wild scene in which a brawling river gathers strength. Here is a landscape of rocks, heather and bog-cotton.

The Hodder, in its lively early stage, is robbed of its spirit by Stocks Reservoir, brought into use in 1932 to serve the thirsty Fylde district of Lancashire. To line the clay of the dam, the contractors opened up Jumbles Quarry.

Catlow Farmhouse.

Today, a footpath running west of the water follows the course of the old narrow-gauge railway which was used to transport the stone. The modern walker passes through forlorn cuttings and leaps across small becks where the rotting remnants of wooden bridges and sleepers may still be found.

In the construction period, when labour was plentiful and cheap, the foreman at the quarry sacked the entire workforce. Engine drivers were instructed not to give any discharged person a lift back to Hollins Village, where most of the men were quartered.

The Hodder is a fishing preserve where anglers try to tempt brown trout. In the pre-reservoir days, salmon ran up the Hodder, many of the fish being poached. A vicar who preached against this practice found, next morning, a salmon was hanging from the sneck of the vicarage door with a note stating: "Tak it and say nowt." He did not preach about poaching again.

The wild cries of several hundred Canada geese impart a wilderness flavour to Stocks Reservoir in winter. The whistling of hundreds of wigeon punctuates the lean days. On the gathering grounds, where sitka spruce grows lustily under a grey Bowland sky are sika and roe deer. In summer, a deafening row comes from the gullery on an island in Stocks which, in the old days, was but a minor hillock near Grange Farm (long since demolished).

Slaidburn village, of Anglian foundation, has an ideal position near where Croasdale Brook joins the Hodder. Slaidburn is drawn out and relatively thin, resembling a letter T with a long stem. An upper room of the thirteenth century *Hark to Bounty Inn* (originally the *Dog Inn* and then named after a specific hound) is still furnished with oak benches and a dock, being once a forest court, dealing with minor offences.

St Andrew's Church has a communion table instead of an altar, in the spirit of the Reformation, and also a three-decker pulpit. On the village green, beside the Hodder, a Victorian maker of "beaver" hats tacked out rabbit skins to dry.

Newton, an important crossing point of the Hodder, has a hotel named after the Parkers, a burial ground used by the Quakers and a relatively modern village hall, where dancers from a wide area enjoy the old steps and tunes. The Hodder flows through a park-like country, passing near Knowlmere Manor, which was built in Victorian times, though the name is linked with Elias de Knoll, who owned the manor in the thirteenth century.

Public footpaths give Knowlmere a wide berth, and I enjoy following a path which leads to a footbridge over the Hodder. This is not the classic Ribble Valley stone arch with parapets but a bridge strung between piers made of brick and concrete. There is a swaying motion during the crossing.

The river is still running clear and cool at Dunsop Bridge, which stands in the grandest part of the Hodder Valley, with well-wooded hills appearing to occupy half the sky. On the green at Dunsop Bridge is a unique payphone—the 100,000th and the most centrally situated in Britain.

The Ordnance Survey, using a mathematical computerised technique, fixed the precise spot as an old barn in the middle of a field at Chadswell Hall Farm, Chaigley, in the Ribble Valley. Pilgrims to the heart of Britain had previously gone to Cromwell's Bridge over the Hodder, two miles away.

The Hodder surges grandly through the gorge at Whitwell and flows under Higher Hodder Bridge, always appearing to me to flow faster the closer it gets to the Ribble! The trees seen on the walk between the bridges are on the grand scale—beech, ash, oak among them—and also present are rowans which offer the late summer spectacle of red berries.

Breaking out from woodland, the path follows a grassy riverbank, ending with entry into a large coniferous wood, where flights of wooden steps indicate where a worn old riverside path was re-routed.

While crossing the Lower Hodder Bridge, there is time to look at the skeletal form of Cromwell's Bridge, once known as "Brig of Hoder" but re-named when, in the summer of 1648, eight thousand of Cromwell's men "crossed Hodder bridge over Ribble." Cromwell wrote: "Last night we lay at Mr Sherburne of Stonehurst." Next day, they intercepted the Royalists at Preston.

Hurst Green and Stonyhurst

Stonyhurst is a noble specimen...with a magnificent gateway, a large hall, with a screen and bow windows, adorned with armorial bearings, a large chamber of state, a gallery and a chapel...all on a grand scale.

T D Whitaker, History of Whalley (1801).

I PREFER the lanquid approach, on foot, from Cromwell's Bridge and beside Hodder and Ribble. At a junction of the road with Stonyhurst is a bus shelter, with a wooden seat, forming an ideal refuge from a sneaky wind as I have a snack or consult the map.

Ignoring the direct route to the College, I cross the road to where the wavy blue emblem of the Ribble Way is displayed beside a stile which gives access to clayey land. The route takes in the yard of Winckley Farm, named after a family who settled here seven centuries ago. The gleam of water is seen, raising hopes that this is a moated farmhouse, but the water is L-shaped, the resort of ducks and, once, the place where Winckley tanners soaked the animal skins.

The path arrives at the edge of the Hodder just before it provides an infusion for the Ribble. Geologists tell us that before the Ice Age re-shaped the district, what became the Hodder was a lusty river with its own valley and that it flowed to the north of Longridge Fell. As the ice melted, boulder clay blocked the old course and the water eroded a new channel, east of the Fell.

Down by the river, farmers are on nodding terms with anglers. The tidy-minded Padiham Club has several well-creosoted open-ended huts with seats, offering shelter from wind and rain on the alluvial flatland where the wind moans around a circular hillock which is referred to on the map as "tumulus."

The walker passes a farm called Jumbles and looks across the newly-merged Ribble and Calder at the handsome seventeenth century facade of Hacking Hall. A public seat on two strong metal supports is one of those provided from the bequest of Jessica Lofthouse, the former librarian, who spent the latter part of her life writing incessantly and with love about her native Ribblesdale. The river birds include goosander, mallard, oystercatcher.

A concessionary path keeps fairly close to the river. I usually follow the direct path to Hurst Green which, set against a backdrop of the Longridge Fells, is spacious and attractive. The architecture ranges from rural cottage to the palatial *Shireburn Arms*.

It is always a pleasure to introduce friends to Stonyhurst College, which has a Catholic foundation. In the district, a visitor is vaguely aware of a grand range of buildings, especially as they occupy a ledge of land beneath Longridge Fell, but lofty deciduous trees obscure the views.

To walk in from Hurst Green to a column supporting a statue of Our Lady, then to turn right, is to see the College in its glorious parkland setting. The Avenue runs as straight as an arrow-shot to a range of buildings of a reddish hue, with stylish towers surmounted by copper domes which have weathered to the hue of verdigris. The range of buildings is vast, but only the central tower, with the south wing and pavilion, belong to Elizabethan times.

Edward I gave "the land of Stanihurst" to Walter Bayley, one of whose descendants married into the illustrious Shireburns, who were a power in the land for four centuries. Their home was extended by Hugh Shireburn (died 1527) and Sir Richard Shireburn who, ten years later, inherited Stonyhurst and re-built the mansion on a grand scale. The impressive West Front is from this period.

My greatest ambition for years was to see one of the treasures: the seventh century gospel of St John which came from the coffin of St Cuthbert, but this was eventually moved for extra safe keeping to London. I recall seeing another curiosity—a table on which (so 'tis said) Oliver Cromwell slept in August, 1648.

Stonyhurst College.

The Shireburns paid dearly for its allegiance to the King during the Civil War. Six members were killed. Cromwell and his army, some 8,000 men, when on a forced march from Knaresborough to intercept a Scottish Army reported to be at Preston, halted at Stonyhurst.

An Army captain reported: "That night we pitched our camp at Stonyares Hall, a Papist house, one Sherburne's." Cromwell is said to have described the uncompleted mansion of the Shireburns as "the finest half-house he had ever seen".

With a fear of assassination, the Protector chose to sleep on a large table, which was moved to the centre of the room. He is said to have kept one eye open and to have had his pistols and sword beside him. He must have slept well, for next day he was clear-headed and his strategy won the day. The Royalists were routed. Cromwell called at Stonyhurst on his return journey.

Sir Nicholas was the man who beautified Stonyhurst by laying out the grounds and setting men to work excavating the rectangular ponds which, when viewed from the park, give the range of buildings an airy appearance which belies the size. His were the Eagle towers, which are major landmarks in the valley.

The Shireburn line died out in 1717; the estates passed to the Welts and (in 1794, through the generosity of Thomas Weld) to the Jesuits at Liege, who had been driven from their establishment by revolution. Stonyhurst did not brood on the past. This was the first public building in England to be illuminated by gas (1811). When Father Joseph Postlethwaite was asked to lecture about it in Preston, there was so much local interest that Preston became the first provincial town in the country to adopt the new type of lighting.

Around Pendle Hill

When Pendle Hill doth wear a hood
Be sure the day will not be good.

Old weather couplet.

Pendle...a vast black mountain, which is the morning weather glass of the country people.

Stukeley (1725).

NO self-respecting witch would use the windy plateau of Pendle as a landing strip, though popular imagination and much written work associates Lancashire's best-known hill with witches.

Visitors to the "witch country" expect to see Chattox or Demdike in flight. Wearing their best black clothes and high hats, they zoom across the hill on their broomsticks with the verve of RAF jet aircraft on low-flying manoevres. I doubt if those old cronies could have jumped over a broomstick, much less flown one. The witches belong to the farms and villages around the hill. Pendle itself is left to the sheep and a few moor birds.

With an elevation of only 1,832 ft (557m), it's not quite a mountain, but this hill crowns the view for those living in the Ribble Valley and the string of Lancashire industrial towns which, at night, are aglow with sodium chloride street lighting, ensuring that the hilltop is never truly dark.

Pendle looks to some like a ridge tent, with one pole shorter than the other. It has also been compared with the hull of a boat, resting upside down. From Downham, the Big End o'Pendle fills half the sky. Seen from across the valley, such as Kemple End, it is a long ridge. Those who climb to the top find, to their amazement, that they cannot straddle it, as a rider on a horse; they find themselves on a breezy plateau. Pendle is, in essence, a Pennine flat-top.

Pendle Hill.

This big, bare hill and its environs were well-wooded, to judge by the remains of former trees preserved in the claggy peat. Dr Spencer T Hall, a Victorian writer with an imposing name, concluded: "There must be something very antiseptic in the earth near Pendle, or in its water...since in Twiston Moss, oak, fir and ash trees, with hazel amongst them which had not yet cast their nuts, have been found, and which must have been there for ages."

The quickest way up Pendle is from Barley—more precisely, the highroad between Barley and Four Lane Ends where, near Pendleside, there is space for roadside parking. A slithery track was reinforced with stones to provide a durable way—a stone staircase—leading almost to the summit cairn. Pendle is the playground of joggers, ramblers, bird-watchers and enthusiasts for hang-gliding. I have also seen grannies, hosts of small children, a woman wearing shoes with stiletto heels and a small group of nuns.

On Hallowe-en, when the witches are said to be most active, people holding torches ascend Pendle with the idea of being on the summit by midnight. None of the witch-watchers has been reported missing. The witch story, this early seventeenth century account of Pendlesiders tried and executed at Lancaster for practising witchcraft, has a powerful hold on the imagination.

The mid-nineteenth century was a good time for witch-spotters, who felt their spines chilling while turning the pages of William Harrison Ainsworth's melodrama, *The Lancashire Witches—A Romance of Pendle Forest*. Ainsworth's description of the view from Pendle's Big End was not flattering enough to be used in modern tourist brochures. He wrote: "Dreary was the prospect on all sides. Black moor, bleak fell, straggling forest, intersected with sullen streams as black as ink, with here and there a small tarn, or moss-pool, with waters of the same hue."

Walter Bennett, a Burnley historian, wrote what was possibly the first straight history of the Pendle Witches in 1976. Most writers on the subject, including myself, have been inspired by his researches. I look back with pleasure on the odd occasions when I discussed the subject with him at his home.

He would outline the popular idea of a witch-woman who had sold her soul to the Devil and, accompanied by an evil spirit in the shape of a cat or dog, "could cast spells, raise storms, ride through the skies on a broom-stick...and had the power to kill or maim men and cattle." Often she was pictured "dancing round a seething cauldron of loathsome brew or maliciously making clay images of the people she wished to kill."

Walter Bennett then gently pointed out that a so-called witch was usually a withered old woman, often mentally deranged or disfigured by some physical malformation. She was feared for her reputed evil powers. Children fled at her approach.

The researches of Bennett and others have meant that whereas Old Demdike and Old Chattox retain the traditional character, the supporting characters were greatly influenced by Harrison Ainsworth's romantic novel and by Robert Neill's *Mist over Pendle* which, Neill once told me, had been written partly to relieve the boredom when he was serving in the Navy in the remote and lonely situation of the Northern Isles.

(Neill humorously added that when his novel was published, one of the booksellers of the Pendle area would not take a supply until he had read a copy and assured himself he had "got his facts right").

Just forty years after the witch trials came the dawn of a period of enlightenment. George Fox, founder of the Quaker Movement, ascended Pendle in 1652: "And soe wee passed on warning people as wee mett ym of ye day of ye Lorede yt was comeinge upon ym & as wee went I spyed a great high hill cal-ed Pendle Hill & I went on ye toppe of it with much adoe...I was moved to sounde ye day of ye Lorde & ye Lorde lett me see...in what places hee had a great people."

Pendle Hill is divided into moors. The traditional sheep were

Lonks a breed favoured by the hill farmers of the lower Pennines. Now the Lonk blood has been blended with that of the Swaledale breed. Walls are absent from the higher parts of Pendle. The heaf-going instinct of the sheep, whereby each stock tends to keep to its own patch of ground, is cherished.

A shepherd who looked after the sheep on the Barley side of Pendle had a special duty at haytime, when the hill blocked a view of the western sky. He would sit on the hilltop, within sight of the haymakers, and wave a black flag if storm clouds were gathering in the west, giving his fellows two hours' notice of bad weather.

It is possible to circumnavigate Pendle Hill by car, though a motorist needs strong nerves on the narrowest roads. Downham is a good starting point if only to have the "backdrop" of the Big End of Pendle. A local saying declares that if you can see Pendle, it's going to rain and if you cannot see Pendle—it's raining!

Barley has an information centre, ample car parking and facilities for picnicing. Nearby Roughlee Hall, which has an inscribed stone dated 1536 high on the front wall, was the home of Alice Nutter, who was included among the Pendle Witches but was not the witchly type. Could this wealthy, gentle woman, with her strong Catholic faith, have been attending an illegal Mass and, unwilling to incriminate her friends, allowed herself to be thought of as a witch?

Newchurch-in-Pendle (which dates back to the sixteenth century) has a tower which features a curious stone formation, said to represent the all-seeing eye of God. That at least was the opinion of a Catholic priest who, with Dalesman Jim (Jim Fishwick of Chatburn), conducted me through this area twenty-five years ago.

The so-called "witches grave", which is close to the church, is simply the last resting place of one of the many members of the local Nutter family. The parish council noticeboard in the village features the name Goldshaw, one of the five booths of the old forest.

Industrialised Sabden also had treacle-mining as a more unusual local industry. The Sabden Treacle Miners have been harnessed to the local tourist industry. There is talk of them being given a television series. An old, old story relates that local people used to weave parkin, using oatmeal as the warp and treacle as the weft.

A road over the Nick of Pendle passes within a short distance of the Pendle Ski Club's two "dry" slopes, which are situated closes to the *Wellsprings Hotel.* Hang-gliders and kites are flown in this breezy area. A short walk up the Moor Lane from Wiswell brings a visitor to another outstanding fair-weather view of the Ribble Valley, from Kemple End to Penyghent and Fountains Fell.

On the way back to Downham, it is pleasant to call at Worston, which elects a sham Mayor. A prehistoric burial site was found on Worsaw Hill. At a cottage named Crow Hill I was once shown a circular window, said to be a witches' window, which did not seem likely. Witchly happenings occurred on the other side of Pendle Hill.

Worston has its own fantasy world. Associated with the *Calf Head Hotel* was a mock Corporation which elected the sham Mayor, who paid sham debts with prodigious sham cheques drawn on an equally sham bank. The coat of arms of this curious Corporation was adorned by a calf's head. The motto was "Brains Will Tell".

The sham Mayor idea survives to this day, with much effort being put into raising money for charity.

Mining at Rimington

The local woods have fascinating names—Mutton
Acre, Torrid Bank and Hell Hole.

*A Walker's Guide to Bowland
and Pendle (1993).*

RIMINGTON straggles alongside a road, with far-away views
and a famous clothing shop, Cosgroves, as a principal attrac-
tion. Years ago, visitors had their attention claimed by the last
windmill to operate in Ribblesdale. Wind power was used to
activate machines at a saw mill.

One of the hush-hush enterprises of the Tudor period was a
lead mine at Skeleron (or Skelhorn), to the south of Rimington,
from which came lead with a high silver content—twenty-six
pounds of silver to the ton. It was mined surreptiously by
William Pudsay.

According to the historian Webster, William "did get good
store of Silver Ore and converted it to his own use (or rather
coined it as many believe...which the people of that Country
call Pudsay's Shillings to this day). But whether way soever it
was, he precured his pardon for it, and had it, as I am certified
from the mouths of those that have seen it...

"So cunning are the miners that if they find any Vein of Ore
that may contain so much silver as would make it a Mine Royal,

they will not let it be known, but presently beat it, and mix it with their softer Ore, pretending the one will not melt without the other, being with them a common trick, lest their work should be taken from them.''

Pudsay should have declared his mine, which would have led to its forfeiture. His was not the only mine to be worked illegally, but Pudsay cheekily used silver from his mine to coining shillings marked with an escallop, which was the Tower Mint mark for the years 1584, 65 and 86. No Pudsay shilling has been identified as such, for obvious reasons: every effort was made to copy the national coinage exactly. What happened to Pudsay has been related under ''Bolton-by-Bowland''.

These mines were worked fitfully over a long period, the latest attempt to open them up being made in 1920. After about eighty tons of barite had been recovered, work ceased. The disturbed ground sports many species of flower, including harebell, herb robert and thyme.

The name Rimington was given to a famous hymn tune by its composer, who was native born. He set the tune to the words of Isaac Watts, beginning *Jesus shall Reign Where'er the Sun*... Francis Duckworth lived at Rimington for only five years, moving with his parents to nearby Stopper Lane, where they took over the village stores and post office.

These were adjacent to the Wesleyan chapel, the musical centre of the district, where—there being no organ—the hymn-singing was accompanied by an orchestra. The players attended by-weekly practices at various farmhouses.

It was in the grocer's shop, early one Monday morning, that young Francis Duckworth received the inspiration to write his great hymn tune, though he was not aware of it at the time. Many years went by before he put pen to paper.

He was to recall that Monday morning because his Uncle

John, a farmer, entered into a debate with father on the merits of hymn writers. Uncle John who liked the old hymn writers, particularly Isaac Watts, promptly stood at the centre of the shop floor and, in a rich, fervent voice he recited the line "Jesus shall Reign Where'er the Sun".

Uncle added: "Do you know what that means? It means that everybody, everywhere, is going to accept Him. Watts said more in that line than many of your modern verse writers say in a whole hymn." Francis Duckworth was to remember the look on Uncle's face as, with hand uplifted, he spoke so emphatically about the spread of Christianity.

Young Francis Duckworth became organist at Stopper Lane and, on moving to Colne—where he developed a small grocery shop into a successful wholesale business—he became organist at the Albert Road Methodist Church, playing that organ for more than forty years.

He recalled Uncle John's fervency in the shop at Stopper Lane, and received additional inspiration from hearing W H Jude play on a French Mustel organ at Colne, as he sat down to write *Rimington,* which was used for the first time in the Colne Whitsuntide processions of 1904. The words were particularly appropriate to overseas missions; the beauty of the tune was an inspiration to Victorian congregations, and so the composition quickly went round the world.

A friend of Francis Duckworth who heard the tune being played on the gramophone of a Cornish prospector in British Columbia described it as "the melody which expresses the soul of the Pennine people."

Whalley and the Calder

That Whalley is such a lively little place is due entirely
to its position at the meeting of modern highroads.

Jessica Lofthouse (1946).

WHALLEY was by-passed but continues to be a busy place.
This village of four thousand people, scenically dominated by
a 600 ft Nab, has the feel of a small town. The community spirit
is evident in the run-up to Christmas, when a host of visitors
join local people for a pageant, *Pickwick Night,* which evokes
the Victorian days.

A busy roundabout is the centrepoint for traffic which, in the
old pre-by-pass days, was heavy, with much coming-and-
going along a route using the Aire Gap, where several valleys
meet to provide a missing link to the Pennine Chain.

At Whalley, before the by-pass (the greatest visual change to
the Valley since glacial times), traffic moved in fits and starts at
the dictates of coloured lights. Heavy lorries breathed smoke
into the air as their engines idled. In summer, the holiday traffic was unbelievably heavy. Fretful children with buckets and
spades and thoughts about Blackpool Sands stared at the red
light, willing it to change to green.

Whalley's more easy-going present has the assurance which
comes from a millenium of rich and varied history. Nothing

103

seems to take the folk of Whalley by surprise. Everything has a long historical perspective. Even the cricket field is something special, being the venue of the first "Roses" match between Lancashire and Yorkshire.

The late Jimmy Fell contributed 1,100 articles on local topics to the *Clitheroe Advertiser* without giving the impression of being repetitive. Jimmy, when asked about the derivation of the name Whalley would smile and mention the numerous theories and variations in spelling, adding that the one generally accepted is "Well Lea", or field of wells.

Bronze Age folk had a settlement on Clerk Hill. The Romans came this way, and the line of their road from Ribchester to Ilkley forms part of the present parish boundary—a parish once so vast that it extended from Ribble to Rochdale.

Whalley, this lively community by the River Calder, has well over 1,000 years of Christian worship built into its history. Three Celtic-Scandinavian stone crosses in the churchyard—one of them associated with Paulinus—relate to the tenth century and an early phase of north-country Christianity when there was no church as such and the Word was spread by nomadic preachers.

Paulinus not only preached—he baptised. The crosses at Whalley are close to the river, in which the baptisms took place. Strange inscriptions on the crosses so bemused the local people that a story gained credence that anyone who translated them would acquire the knowledge to make themselves invisible!

For centuries, the church, the "White Church under the Leigh", would be a simple, thatched, wooden structure. The present edifice dates from about 1200. On my visits I feel a chill on passing the thirteenth century coffins cut from living rock.

John Wigglesworth, whose earthly remains are in a box-type

Above: Whalley Abbey.
Below: Parish Church of St. Mary and All Saints.

tomb near the south porch, has his virtues recorded in stone. He was "for more than fifty years the principal innkeeper in this Town, withstanding the Temptations of that dangerous Calling, he maintained Good Order in his House, kept the Sabbath Day Holy, frequented the Public Worship with his Family, induced his guests to do the same."

Whalley church, which is kept locked when there is no supervision—a wise precaution because of the lawless minority—is one of my favourite parish churches, with its fourteenth century screen, handsomely-carved choir stalls made for the Abbey about 1430 and brought here at the Dissolution and a heraldic window, featuring (among many) Townley de Townley, Parker de Browsholm (their crest being a trio of deer heads), Assheton, Nowell and Starkie (de Huntroyd).

The misericord carvings hint at the medieval sense of humour, one being of a farrier attempting to shoe a goose and another of a wife belabouring her soldier husband with what looks like a frying pan.

Mention of an Abbey deserves a prompt explanation. The pious folk of Whalley must have stared in disbelief when, at the end of the thirteenth century—six long centuries after their parish church had been founded—a community of monks arrived from Stanlow in Cheshire. These were Cistercian monks, clad in white undyed wool. They took over land granted to them by Henry de Lasci, a descendant of the man who endowed their original house at Stanlow.

At first lodging with the Rector of Whalley, the Cistercians soon set about building the Abbey with gritstone hewn from the Nab and, later, with stone from Simonstone, four miles away.

The Cistercian monks had a special aptitude for sheep farming. The weir seen above the bridge at Whalley has evolved from one made by the monks to divert water along a race to turn the wheel at the Abbey's cornmill. There would be rejoicing along the banks of the Calder when the salmon and sea trout were running.

Whalley Abbey had all the medieval grandeur, with notable guests for whom food was cooked in a kitchen equipped with three big open fireplaces. The cooks dealt with gargantuan meals, featuring oxen, sheep, calves, lambs, porkers, wild birds and much more. Thomas Johnson, a Victorian writer, calculated that at the period of its greatest prosperity, the mean consumption of the abbey in wine was eight pipes, or 960 gallons per annum, besides white wine—about a bottle a day to each monk.

After listing the large number of animals slain to provide food, he concludes: "The total number of mouths was 120, exclusive of visitors and poor persons who were daily partakers of the monks' hospitality. Certainly those mouths must have been well employed. Nor could so large a proportion of animal food have been anything but detrimental to heath. Fasting would indeed be necessary from time to time, if only to gain an appetite."

John Paslew, the last Abbot, and builder of the splendid Abbot's House, is said to have had a fiery temper. He certainly concerned himself with controversial issues of the day and became involved in the northern rebellion against the ecclesiastical policy of Henry VIII—an uprising which became known as the Pilgrimage of Grace.

When a general pardon was proclaimed in 1536, he did not heed the warning. Paslew, and others, were taken to Lancaster, convicted of high treason and hanged, drawn and quartered in the following year. Whitaker, the historian (a stone effigy of whom can be seen on his tomb in Whalley church) quoted a local tradition that Paslew was brought back to Whalley to be hanged.

The Crown took over the Abbey, removing lead from the roof. The monks dispersed. The aged last Prior of Whalley, one Christopher Smith, was allowed to remain in the village and he died, a sad man, in 1539.

Happily for Whalley, only eight years after Paslew's death the Abbey had come into the possession of Richard Assheton and Thomas Bradyll. Assheton, buying out Bradyll, moved into the old Abbot's lodgings. In 1588, the premises were converted into a splendid house which was grandly extended in 1694. Meanwhile, in about 1660, Sir Ralph Assheton had the Abbey Church "unbuilt" [dismantled]. Good use would be found for the stone.

Having fallen into a state of disrepair by 1836, the remains of Whalley Abbey were sold to John Taylor, a calico painter of Whalley; he willed it to John Hargraves, who restored the buildings in accordance with the Gothic style popular in the mid-nineteenth century. The property is now the Blackburn & Diocesan Conference and Retreat House, which is available for conferences, private celebrations and bed and breakfast. "The House is licensed and 100 guests can be seated in the Dining Hall."

Whalley Abbey thus continues the monastic tradition of providing hospitality for staying guests and also day-trippers, there being a gift shop, tea and coffee shop and a picnic area. Nostalgia was being catered for by Wendy's Memory Lane exhibition (separate admission charge).

The original heavy doors adorn the north-east gate, making it easily possible to imagine the coming and going of Abbots, monks and distinguished medieval visitors. The North-West Gateway, an early fourteenth century structure spanning the old road to Ribchester, provides the historically-minded with a splendid medieval feature.

The driver of a car passes from the cool greyness of this ancient structure to see a railway viaduct ("Whalley arches"), of vivid (one writer wrote "vulgar") red bricks, made on site, and completed in 1852. Counting the arches is not easy because of the length of the structure; there are officially forty-nine.

Over Whalley Arches passed some of the early diesel locomotives to be used by British Rail; the Blackburn to Clitheroe run proved to be most suitable for testing. Not far away is an example of modern bridge-building using concrete—a bridge which carries the Whalley-Clitheroe by-pass over the Calder.

At Billington, on my way to visit the confluence of the Calder and Ribble, I found a good vantage point and looked far across the Valley to the Bowland fells. Also in view, rising above the trees, were the cupolas of Stonyhurst College.

I was entering Jessica Lofthouse Country, if I may term it thus. Her prolific career as an author was launched with the publication in 1948 of *Three Rivers*, "being an account of many wanderings in the dales of Ribble, Hodder and Calder".

"Big Ribble" was broad and deep after assimilating "the clear Hodder" and "poor Cinderella Calder which comes sliding in a sinister flood under the beautiful woods beyond Mitton Point." Substantial public seats paid for by the Jessica Lofthouse bequest are to be found in this district.

Having seen the huge facade of seventeenth century Hacking Hall from across the Ribble, I was keen to go closer. Jessica mentioned the old Hacking boat which ferried people across the Ribble. In her day, the boat might be tantalizingly near but the boatman was unable to hear the calling and whistle of one person. His hearing improved when several travellers were assembled, waiting to cross.

William Palmer, another writer about the Ribble Valley, whistled shrilly. In due course, the ferryman arrived, telling Palmer he must consider himself lucky. He [the boatman] had been about to go to bed when the whistle blew "and then he would not have moved to our aid." For many years, the chief customers of the ferry were priests of Stonyhurst who used the crossing as a short cut between their school chapel and places on the Langho side of the river where services were held.

In my quest for Hacking Hall, I turned off the main road to pass between a Roman Catholic High School and a war memorial. Elke Lane (formerly Eller Carr, a place where alder grew) was asphalted at first, then became a roughish track. Hacking Hall was partly obscured by a brick building but, nonetheless, rose majestically above the fields near the confluence of Ribble and Calder.

At Potterford, I heard that this placename was derived from the use of local clay—a hard blue clay—for making into pots at Chew Mill. The suffix "ford" is self-evident. Here, on the higher ground, after a wet spell, the exposed earth is glutinous. I thought of it as Copydex Country after the famous adhesive.

I decided to walk for the last few hundred yards to Hacking Hall and, under the scrutiny of a big sheepdog called Bess, I reached a magnificent edifice named after a medieval family who resided at Hacking when the hall stood on a platform and was encircled by a moat. The flats near the two rivers are sandy, in marked contrast to the clay of higher ground.

The present tenants of this farm on the Duncan Halgh Estate recalled when the moat re-appeared with flooding from the rivers. In 1978-9 and in 1984, the occupants were "marooned", the water lapping over the approach road to a depth of a foot. In the 1960s, here and at other places along the river, farmers came across lordly salmon which were "flapping about" on the river bank when the water had receded.

From the Hackings, a medieval hall passed to the Shuttleworths, thence (via a heiress and in marriage) to the Walmesleys of Dunkenhalgh. The Elizabethan Judge Walmesley, the new owner of the estate, had the home of his wife's family pulled down and the present Hall built in 1607.

The big old cruck barn, standing a quarter of a mile away, is where the Hacking Hall cattle are milked. I noticed with some amusement a variant of the now traditional black plastic bag for silage, this being a bag with alternating black and white stripes, giving the appearance of a gigantic humbug.

The Roman road from Ribchester crossed the land at what is now the front of the house—a working farmhouse, presiding over a hundred acres of ground. Indoors are the usual big living rooms and kitchen, with two inglenooks, plus seven bedrooms, two landings and two staircases, with an attic running the full length of the house. Some upper windows were blocked off at the time of the unhygenic tax on window space.

The cattle at Hacking Hall are milkers, being Friesian crossed with Holstein. The half-bred sheep are Blue-faced Leicester crossed with Swaledale. A Suffolk tup is put to them to produce lambs for meat production. When I was last at Hacking, in late January, lambing time was under way and two newborn lambs, jet black as opposed to the more common mottled lambs, were bleating for milk.

The angling interests are paramount. Here are some of the most famous salmon pools—Hacking Boat, Jumbles, Pea Scar and Luke Lum as far as an aqueduct, then Raid Deep, Trows, Addison's Stream, Millstone Hole and Sale Wheel.

The Jumbles, just below the line which was taken by the Hacking ferry, was a name derived from the noise made by the

Ribble as it surged over a rocky bed. Sale Wheel, which has been described as "the last picturesque portion of the Ribble", is where, after flowing through a rock channel, the Ribble widens and sweeps around the base of a small hill known as The Haugh. Various writers have warned visitors of "strong undercurrents".

A heron was in ponderous flight. Mink are seen beside both Calder and Hodder, where many years ago otters were relatively common. I heard of local field drains which had been fitted with metal grids, which meant that the drains could not be used for refuge by otters on hunting days.

Nineteenth century industrialisation transformed the Calder and its tributaries. Draining deep, narrow valleys, they began to convey sludge and waste products from the mill towns. Pollution from gas works and print works at Low Moor and Barrow respectively had an immediate effect on the Ribble.

When a six week's drought ended with a thunderstorm over Church and Oswaldtwistle in June, 1859, the whole of the refuse matter poured into the greatly shrunken Hyndburn, Calder and Ribble, where "the dense black mass" killed all the fish for six miles, "chiefly trout, flukes and eels, but a few salmon."

Organic matter coming down the Calder settled and rotted in the mill dam at Whalley. The occasional serious flood washed the dam clean—and sent a black flood into the Ribble to the detriment of the fishery.

In 1860, a Commission heard of refuse from Accrington, Church and Oswaldtwistle entering the Ribble. Here the trout were found sickly "in consequence of the state of the water; they come to the side and gasp for breath; even cattle at Ribchester suffer."

Today, the National River Authority leads the campaign to

clean up the rivers. In 1994, a farmer living near the outflow of the Calder told me, jubilantly, that—to his knowledge—at least one salmon entered the Calder in 1993.

The Calder at Whalley.

Ribchester

Ribchester is now a poor thing; it hath been an
ancient town...
Leland (c1540).

RIBCHESTER holds in its name a hint of its illustrious past.
The word "chester" means a camp, and where Ribchester now
stands lay the Roman fort of Bremetennacum Veteranorum.
Some say that the pillars supporting the porch at the *White Bull*
are of re-cycled Roman stone.

Chocolate-tinted road signs lead the faithful to the Roman remains, among which a group of jabbering television
archaeologists—the Time Team—rummaged for a Channel 4
documentary in 1993. Watching them digging where their fancy was taken, and against the clock, was entertaining—as it was
intended to be. There was even speculation (unconfirmed) that
Venutius, the Brigantean patriot and enemy of Rome, had links
with Ribchester.

The television film ensured that, for a time, Ribchester would
have an abundance of visitors, resulting in streets being tem-
porarily reduced in width to that of a Roman chariot. Not far
from what is now the main car park, Bronze Age folk buried
their cremated dead in urns. From time to time, bits of Ancient
Ribchester have protruded from the eroded banks of the Ribble.

The Black Death claimed over a hundred lives. In the pre-Industrial age, dozens of clacking handlooms testified to visitors that the local people had found useful employment at home. Howitt (1838) remarked on how plain-looking were the weavers' cottages; "as free from any attempt at beauty or ornament as possible." He also mentioned the mean conditions of the ordinary folk, many of whom lived in hovels, with large families—ten or eleven in some cases—scrabbling about in dirty conditions (a state of affairs not peculiar to Ribchester).

Howitt commented that oatcake was a staple food and the clack and shutter of the handloom was the dominant sound. Children were put to work when they were about twelve years old.

Ribchester became part of the domain of King Cotton. Ribblesdale Mill is now devoted to engineering work. Another mill serves Queen Wool. It's the Roman connection which gives lustre to local history. Thomas Pennant (1773), after mentioning Ribchester's poor state wrote, grandly, that it had been "a great Roman station".

A museum of Roman antiquities, and the excavated remains of a Roman bathhouse (now closed from November to Easter), bear witness to much serious research, plus a desire to capture the imagination of children, as with the chain mail and Roman-type helmets which are among the hands-on exhibits.

Ribchester also has a *Museum of Childhood*. I was amused to see a notice in a house window, proclaiming the birth of a girl child under the heading "Watch Out, Ribchester!" A tearoom offers, among several types of tea, the "English breakfast" variety and also fare which the Roman garrison of Ribchester would surely have enjoyed—warm, buttered crumpets with attendant jar of jam.

The abiding impression of Ribchester is the view of the Ribble

Valley, open, neat and tidy but, in the early days of settlement, a well wooded area. Here I am always conscious of Big Ribble. The view of the river takes in the form of Pendle Hill, sprawling languidly, like a cat before the fire. On another day, there might be snow-dogs howling across Pendle and the normally serene Ribble is a peat-stained torrent flowing bank high.

If Ribchester folk have a nervous twitch it is possibly because their village is the only one to sit on a bank of the Ribble. In Roman times, the river was fordable. In due course, the fickleness of the Ribble led to a goodly part of the Roman fort—and other local structures down the years—being swept away.

Ribchester, a compact military base of rather less than six acres, consisted of long, red-tiled buildings. The fort housed a cavalry troop of about 500 men and their horses. They hailed from various parts of the Empire. In early days, they were Asturians, raised in northern Spain (and doubtless augmented, as time went on, by native men).

In later times, as you will see among the models at the museum, Sarmatian cavalry (from what is now Rumania) gave Ribchester an ability to re-act swiftly to emergencies, using the well-made Roman roads.

This fort by the Ribble was strategically placed at a crossing of the ways, with routes extending northwards to Lancaster, westwards to Lytham, southwards to Manchester and eastwards via Elslack to Ilkley.

In the museum, a model of Roman Ribchester is attached to a wall. A guide book illustration shows the fort's distinctive shape—that of a playing card—superimposed on a modern map of the place. You notice that the Ribble claimed one corner of the complex. It was from the river bank, in 1796, that a group of objects, including an outstanding parade helmet, were recovered. The original helmet is in the British Museum; a

116

replica is on view at Ribchester.

A village history trail was devised by Messrs Hodge and Ridge. The trail begins, as should all journeys-through-time, at the museum, with a glimpse (at the rear) of bits and pieces of Roman granaries. Also within the bounds of the old Roman fort is St Wilfrid's church (a Christian site on or about the spot where the temple of Septimus Severus was to be found). The present structure took shape in the thirteenth century and was two centuries old before the immense tower was constructed. What was once called "an irregular pile" was splendidly restored in 1925.

Beyond the churchyard lie Roman ditch defences in an area where traces of the western gates and corner tower have been found. The walk continues around the playing fields (where once the Roman soldiers paraded).

So much for Rome. The village trail continues into a much more modern Ribchester, a place of continuous change as

Remains of the Roman Bathhouse.

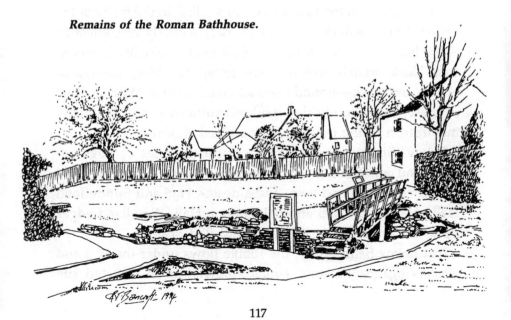

industries and fashions waxed and waned. The cottages made for handloom weavers are fairly common, and the guide mentions that two of those opposite the *White Bull* have "cellar loomshops". (If you would like to pat some Roman stonework, then do so at the four columns supporting the porch of the *White Bull* and take pains not to trip over the stone mounting block).

Walkers on the Ribble Way cannot resist looking round Stydd, near Ribchester. Here is a Roman Catholic church and, tucked away, the ancient Stydd Church, of the twelfth century, connected in its early days with a hospital which was maintained by the Knights Hospitallers. Some attractive early eighteenth century almshouses were built by the Sherbourne family for old and infirm ladies of the Catholic faith.

Ribchester has long been renowned for its "excellent fishing station". A Victorian writer mentioned that "the river is famous for its fine salmon, and many parts of it abound with trout, chub, dace, gudgeon and eels...

"The flies used for salmon vary according to the fancy of the angler; but he will find the plain turkey wing fly very effectual about here; while for trout, the black gnat, drake black, woodcock black, March brown, snipe grey, dun bloe, moorgame brown, and cock-a-bonddu, are all excellent flies. With any one of these, on a cloudy day, with a southern wind, the angler may return to the inn with a good basket of fish..."

Below Ribchester, the river performs a series of huge oxbows and continues to flow through unspoilt country presided over by halls old and new—Osbaldeston Hall and Sunderland Hall, Alston Old Hall and Balderstone Hall. Woodland edges up to the water, as at Will Wife and Red Scar.

Just below Salmesbury, the Ribble flows under the M.6 and washes against Preston, which sprawls on an elevated site known to the Romans. The Ribble Way hugs its northern bank, then switches to the southern bank of a river which now responds to the pulsing of two tides a day.

Each year, lordly salmon nose their way into their natal river and commence a long run to the gravel beds of the upper Ribble, which some of them will reach. Other luckless salmon end up in nets. In 1871, a Preston fishmonger advertised:

> Ribble salmon! Ribble salmon!
> Choicest of the finny tribe.
> Fresh and sparkling from the river,
> Caught with morning's flowing tide.

Old Father Ribble eventually loses himself between goose-haunted marshes. Ribble Wayfarers end or begin their walking at *The Dolphin* Public House beside Longton Marshes, part of the vast Ribble Marshes National Nature Reserve.

Acknowledgements...

George Bargh, Elsie and Billy Barker, Marjorie Calvert, Castle Cement, Clitheroe Information Centre, Clitheroe Public Library, Gisburne Park Private Hospital, Kathleen Douglas, Whalley Abbey, Tony Jackson, Viscount Mills (National River Authority), Ribchester Museum, William Saunders, Bob Swallow, Waddow Hall Guide Centre, James Wilkinson, Jack Wolfenden, Harold Woods, David Yorke, Major J E E Yorke.